A-Z SOUTHERN ENGLAND

Key to Map Pages	2-3
Road Maps	4-42
Town Plans, Airports & Port Plans	43-48
Index to Towns and Villages	49-60

REFERENCE

Motorway	**M3**
Under Construction	
Proposed	
Motorway Junctions with Numbers	
Unlimited Interchange **4** Limited Interchange **5**	
Motorway Service Area (with fuel station) **ROWNHAMS**	Ⓢ
with access from one carriageway only	Ⓢ
Major Road Service Areas (with fuel station)	**SUTTON SCOTNEY**
with 24 hour facilities	Ⓢ
Primary Route (with junction number)	**A33** 19
Primary Route Destination	**POOLE**
Dual Carriageways (A & B Roads)	
Class A Road	**A30**
Class B Road	**B2070**
Major Roads Under Construction	
Major Roads Proposed	
Fuel Station	
Gradient 1:5(20%) & Steeper (Ascent in direction of arrow)	≪
Toll	Toll
Mileage between Markers	8
Railway and Station	
Level Crossing and Tunnel	
River or Canal	
County or Unitary Authority Boundary	
National Boundary	
Built-up Area	
Village or Hamlet	
Wooded Area	
Spot Height in Feet	• 813
Relief Above 400' (122m)	
National Grid Reference (Kilometres)	190
Area Covered by Town Plan	**SEE PAGE 44**

TOURIST INFORMATION

Airport		⊕
Airfield		+
Heliport		Ⓗ
Battle Site and Date		1066 ⚔
Castle (open to public)		▉
Castle with Garden (open to public)		Ⓜ
Cathedral, Abbey, Church, Friary, Priory		✝
Country Park		ⵢ
Ferry (vehicular)		⛴ 🚢
(foot only)		👥
Garden (open to public)		❀
Golf Course	9 Hole 🏌9	18 Hole 🏌18
Historic Building (open to public)		⌂
Historic Building with Garden (open to public)		⌂
Horse Racecourse		🏇
Lighthouse		♨
Motor Racing Circuit		🏁
Museum, Art Gallery		🖼
National Park		
National Trust Property	(open)	NT
	(restricted opening)	NT
Nature Reserve or Bird Sanctuary		🐑
Nature Trail or Forest Walk		🍃
Place of Interest		Monument •
Picnic Site		🪑
Railway, Steam or Narrow Gauge		🚂
Theme Park		🎡
Tourist Information Centre		ℹ
Viewpoint	(360 degrees)	⁂
	(180 degrees)	⁑
Visitor Information Centre		Ⓥ
Wildlife Park		ⵣ
Windmill		⚙
Zoo or Safari Park		🐘

SCALE

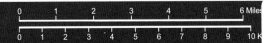

0	1	2	3	4	5	6 Miles

| 0 | 1 | 2 | 3 | 4 | 5 | 6 | 7 | 8 | 9 | 10 K |

T0337525

EDITION 13   2023

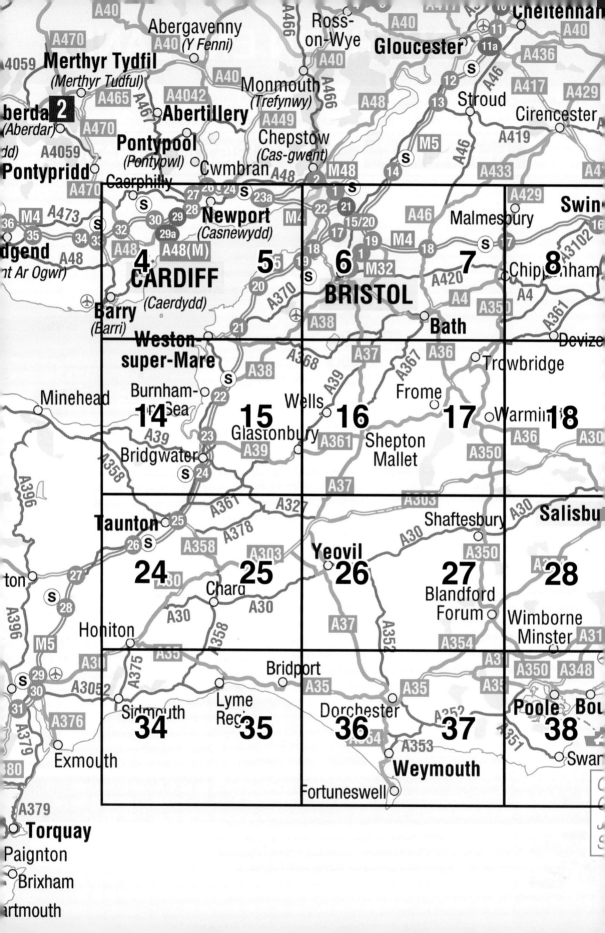

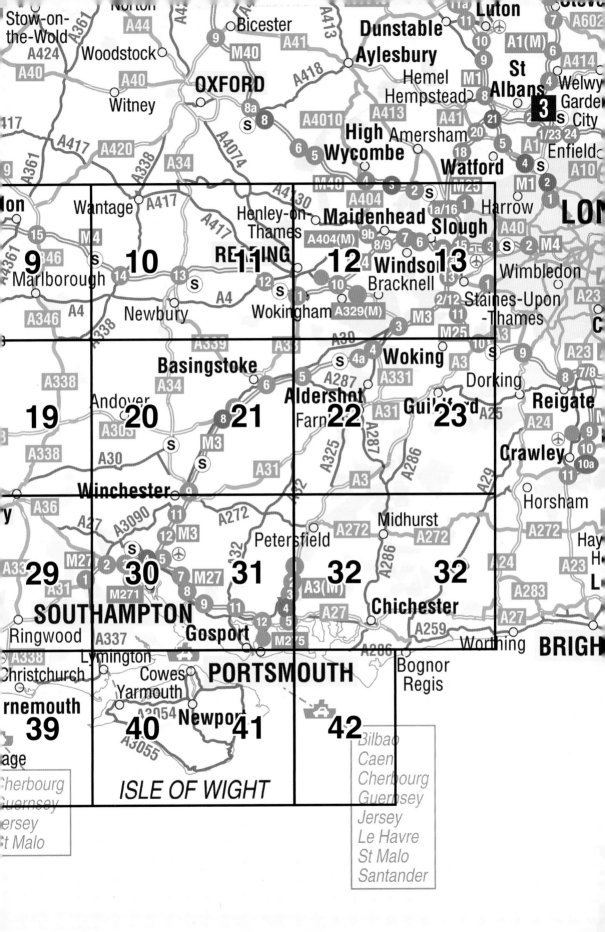

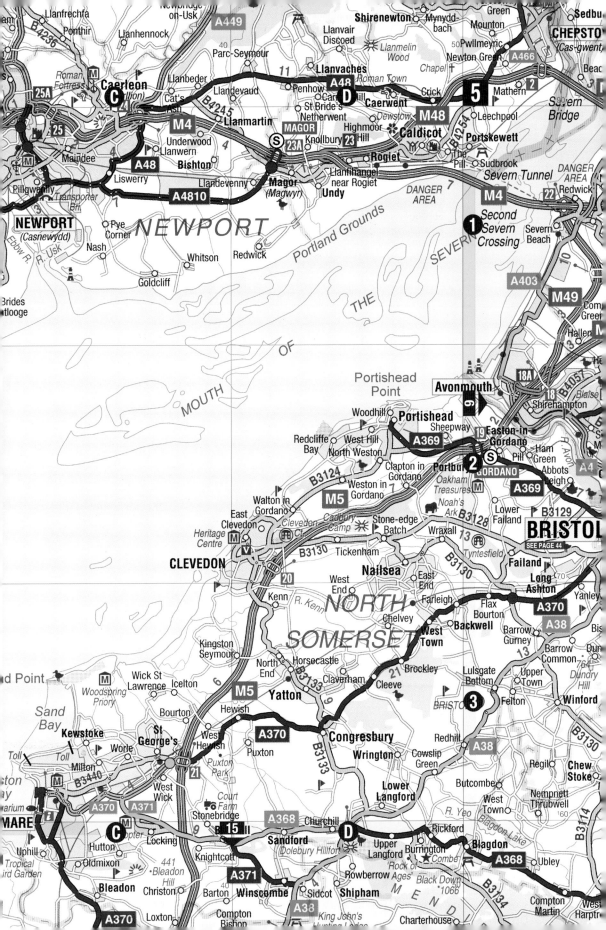

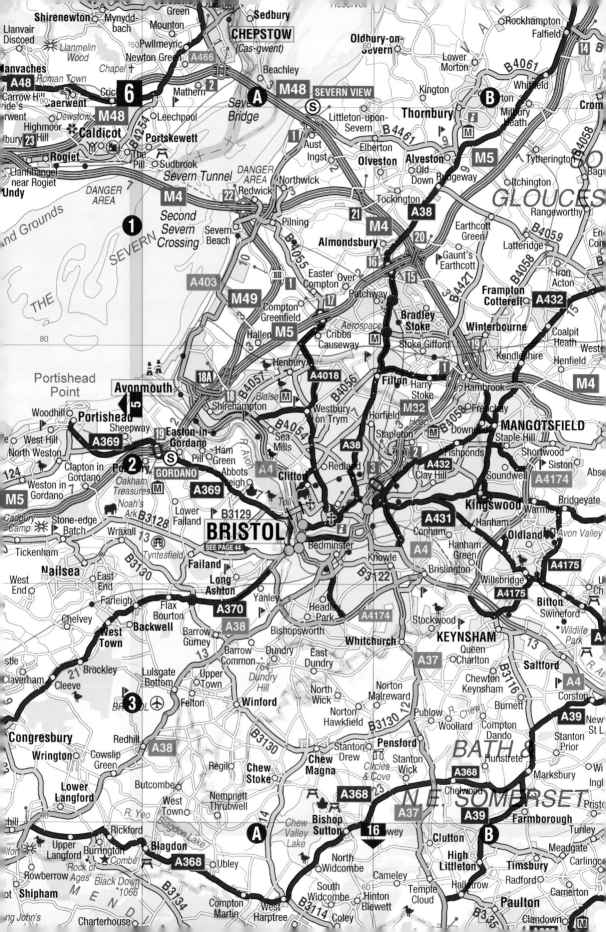

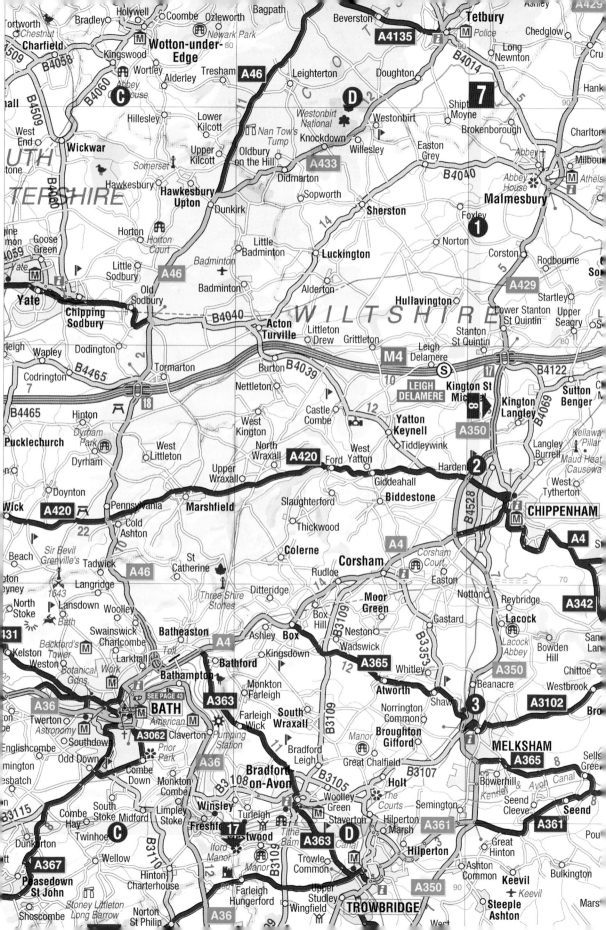

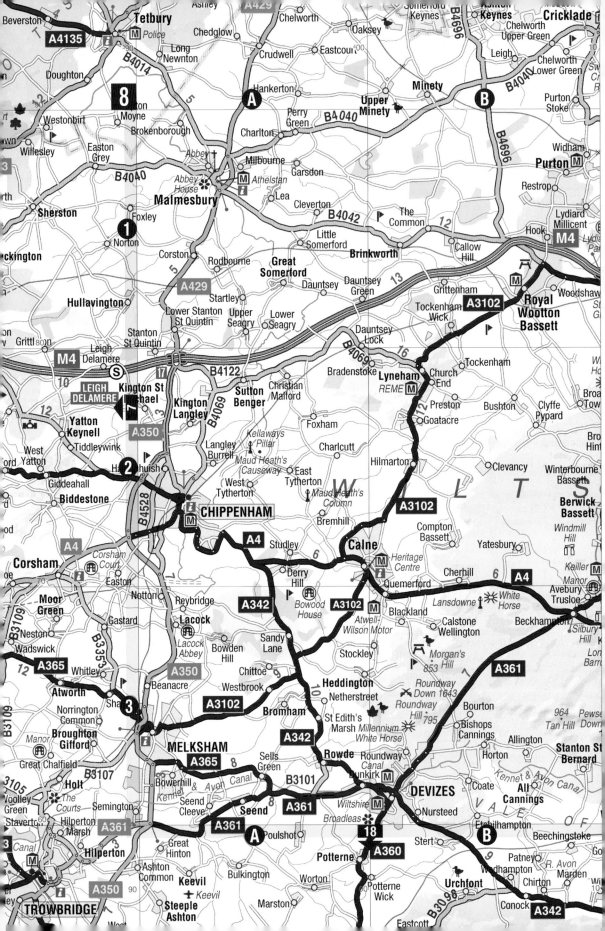

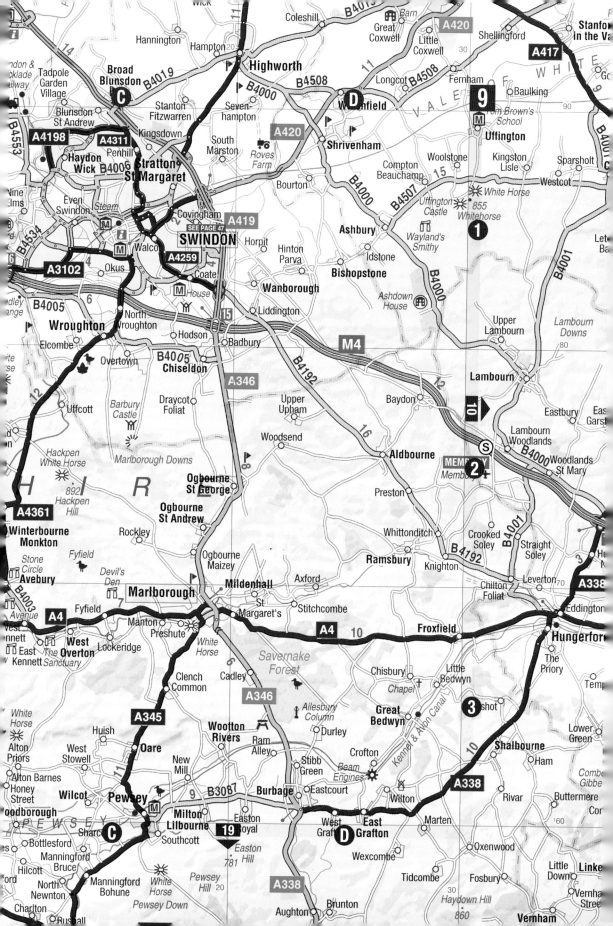

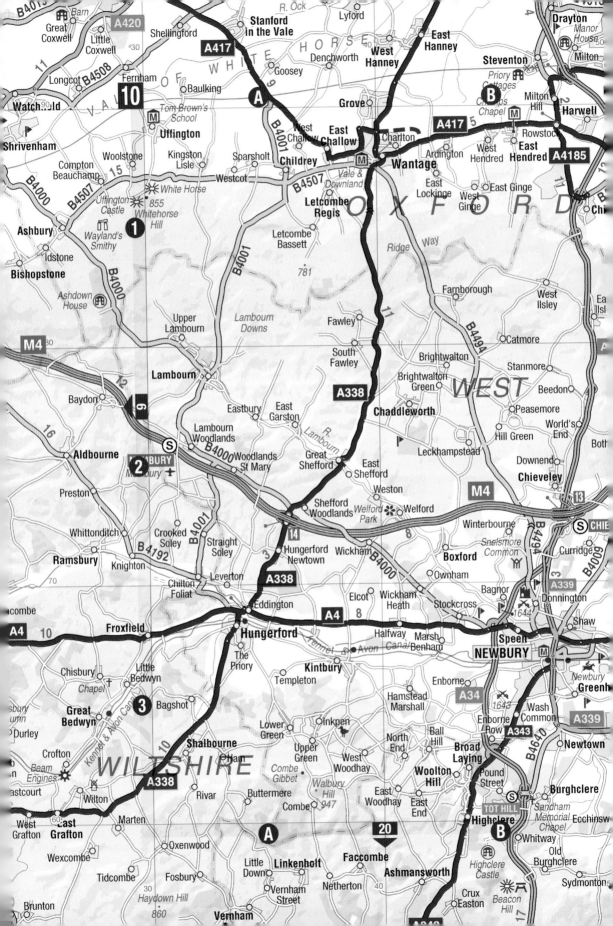

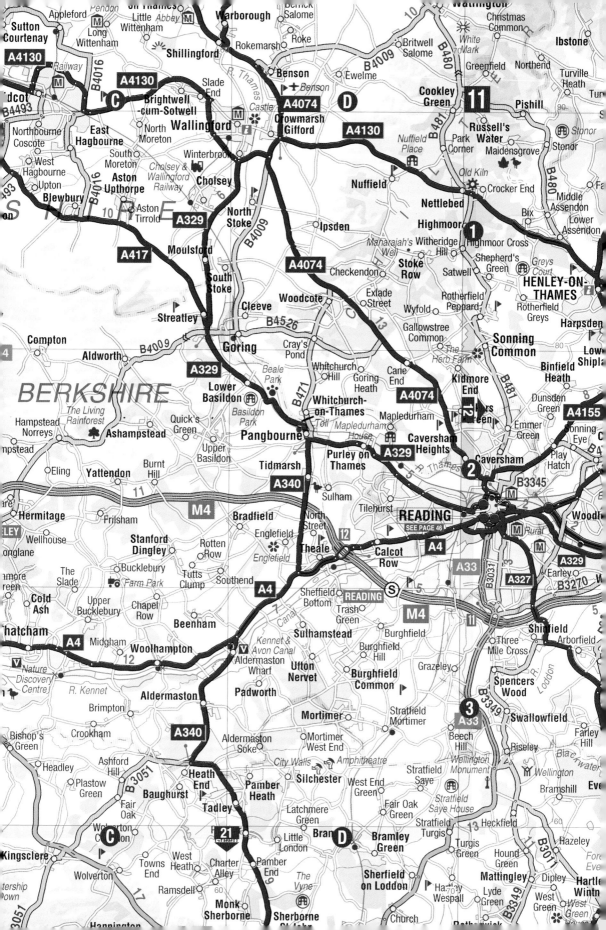

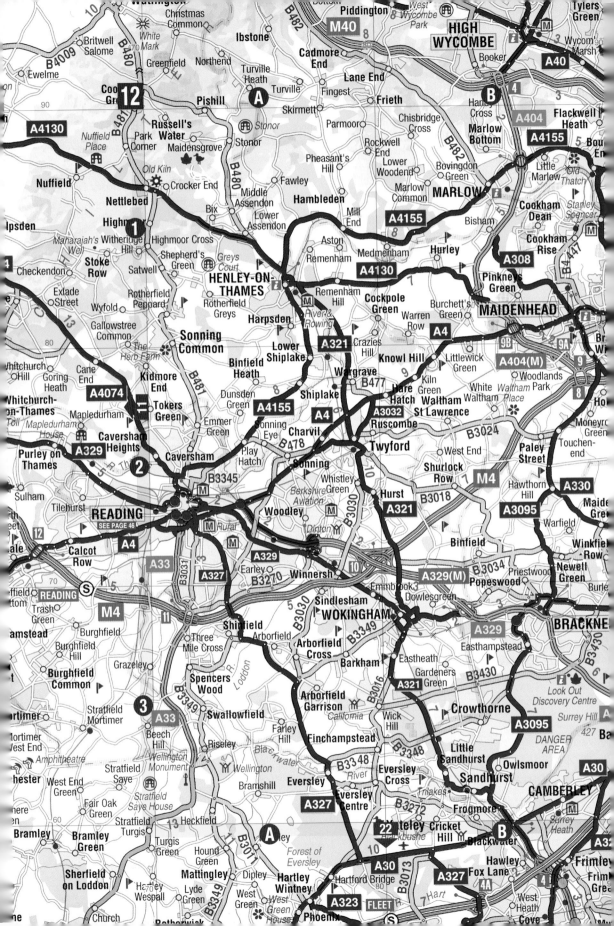

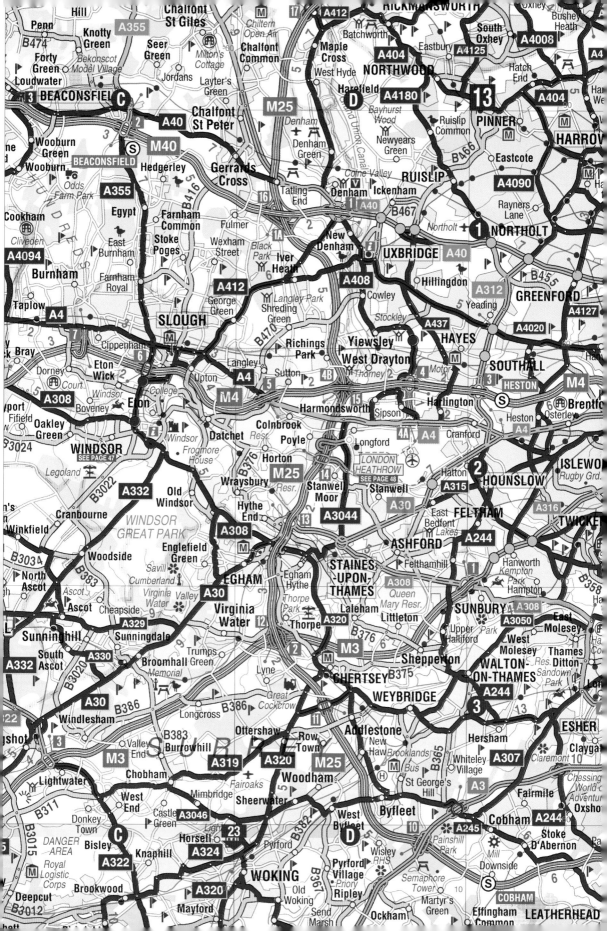

BRISTOL CHANNEL

1

Brean Down Fort

Brean Down

Brean

Brean Leisure Park

Berro

B R I D G W A T E R

B A Y

BURNHAM-ON-S

B3
High

50

chor

2

Power Station

Lilstock

Knighton

Stolford

Steart

Hun
West
Hunts

M **Watchet**
Doniford

East Quantoxhead

Kilton

Burton

Shurton

Wick

Stockland Bristol

Stretcholt

B3191

Five Bells

Kilve

Stringston

Stogursey

Otterhampton

Combwich

Pawlett

Old
leeve   B3190

West Quantoxhead

Dodington

Holford

Fiddington

Coultings

A3

M
Washford
Tropiquaria

Williton

Nether Stowey

Oatley

Rodway

Walled

Chilton Trinity

Abbey
Cider Farm
Torre

Sampford Brett

Bicknoller

Over Stowey

Coleridge Cottage

Cannington

Stream

Capton

Vellow

Newton

Halsway

Aley

Charlynch

Bradley Green

Wembdon

ggearn
uish

Yarde

B3188

Kingswood

1175

Spaxton

Four Forks

Northfield

M

B3190

Monksilver

Chidgley

Stogumber

Crowcombe

Plainsfield

Pightley

Enmore

Blake

M

Combe Sydenham

Elworthy

Higher
oxford

Lower Vexford

Triscombe

Aisholt

Merridge

Durleigh
Resr.

Durleigh

Ham

BRIDGWATER

Elworthy
Cottage

3

Flaxpool

1261
Wills
Neck

Courtway

Goathurst

B3224

1290

Rook's
Nest

Willett

Heathfield

West
Bagborough

Cothelstone

Huntstile

**North
Petherton**

orthy
rvoir

**Lydeard St
Lawrence**

Seven
Ash

Terhill

Fyne
Court

Broomfield

A38

**Brompton
Ralph**

Tolland

Tarr

**Combe
Florey**

15

East
Combe

**Kingston
St Mary**

Shearston

Thurloxton

10

Clatworthy

Pitsford
Hill

30

A

Gauge

**Bishops
Lydeard**

24

Hesterc

B

Adsborough

Langley
Marsh

Whitefield

Ford

Ash
Priors

West
Somerset Railway

M

A358

Nailsbourne

Upper
Cheddon

Cheddon
Fitzpaine

M

**West
Monkton**

We
New

Heydon
Hill

V

Langley

Wiveliscombe

Croford

Fitzhead

Halse

Preston
Bowyer

Cotford
St Luke

Langfor

Staplegrove

Monkton
Heathfield

A3259

Durs

Creech H

**Creech
St Michael**

TAUNTON

Heathfield

Norton
Fitz

Bathpool

200

DEANE

VALE

Milverton

B3227

B3224

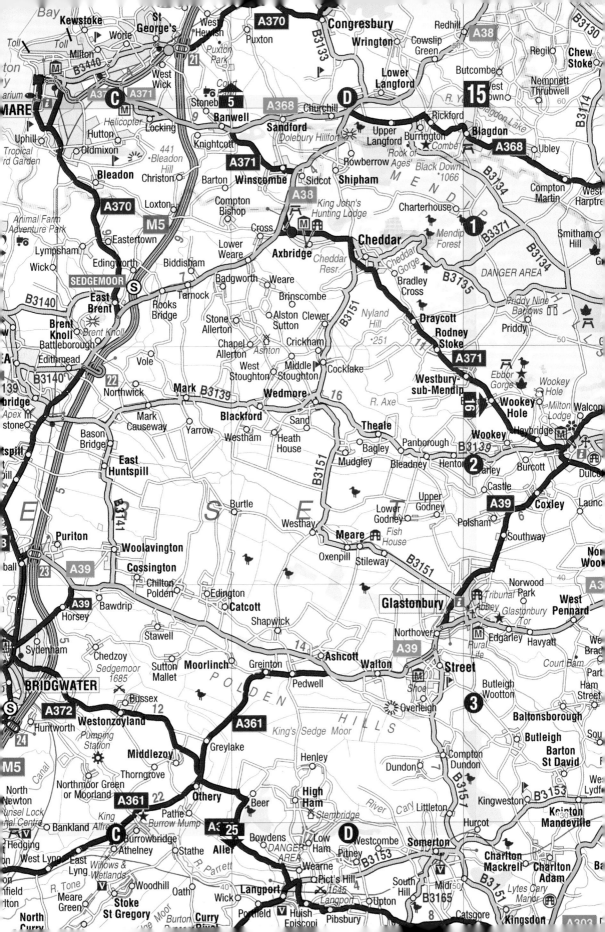

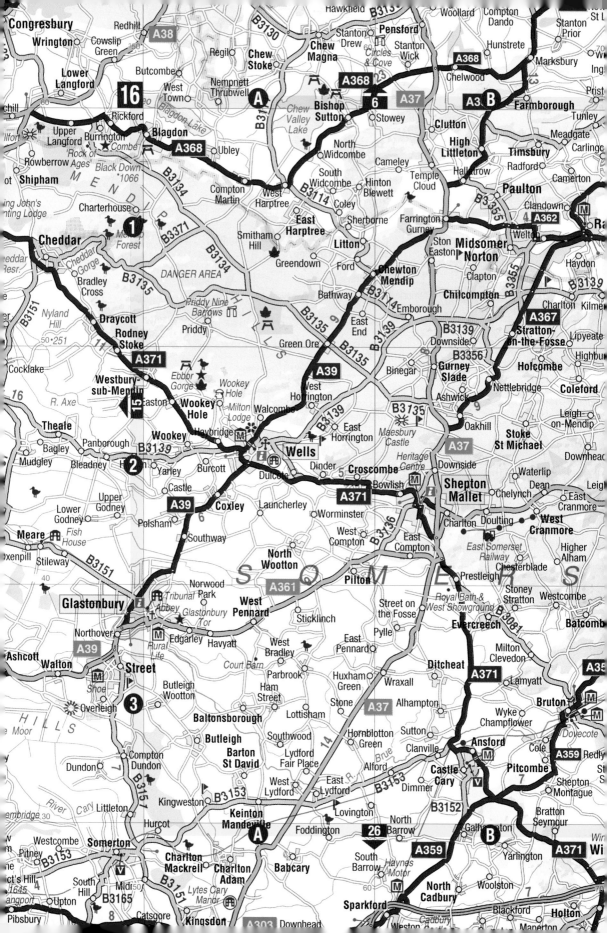

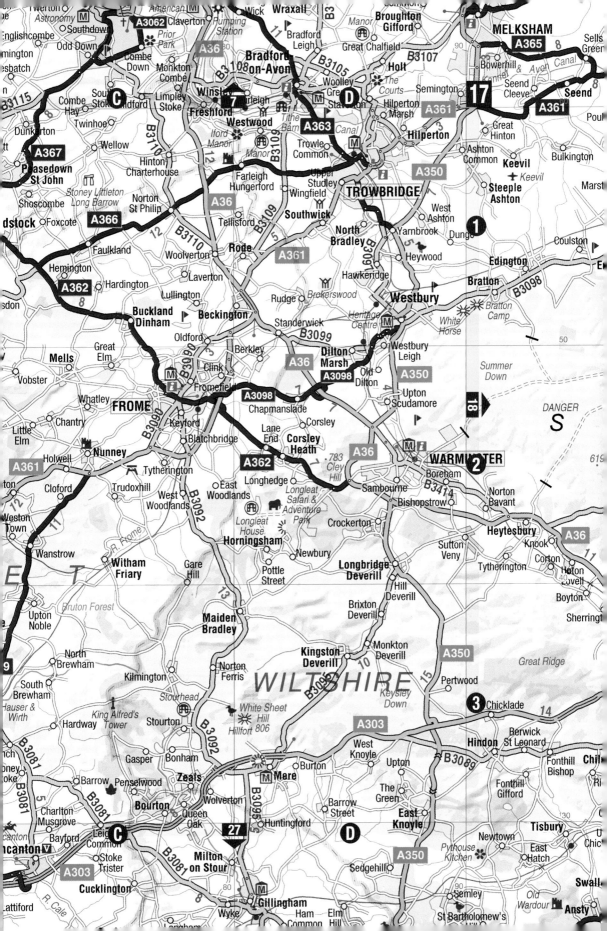

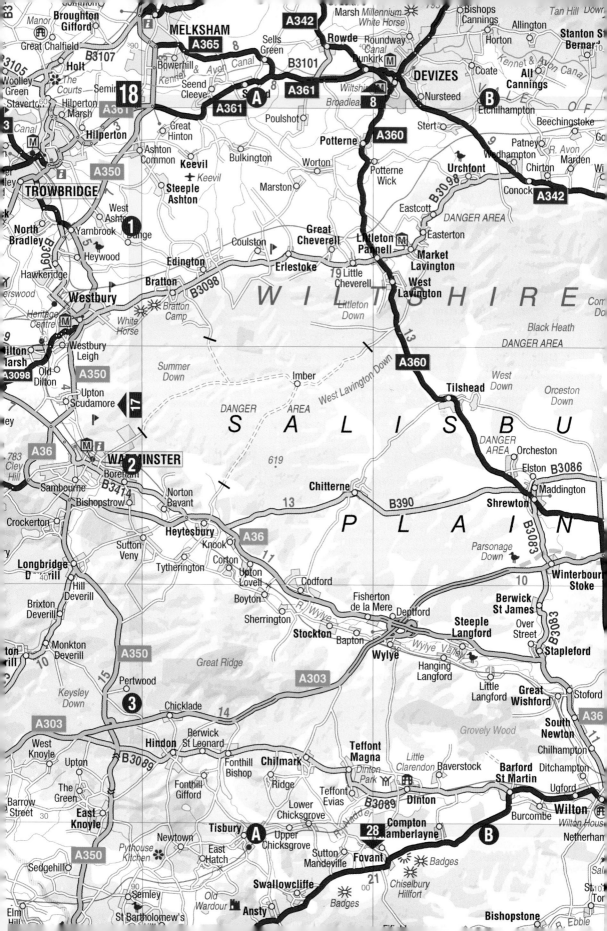

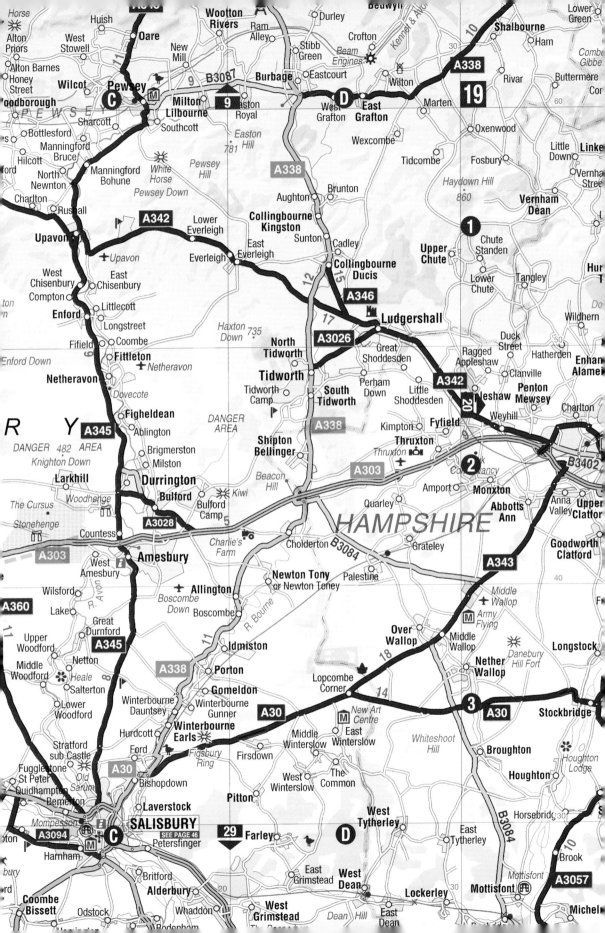

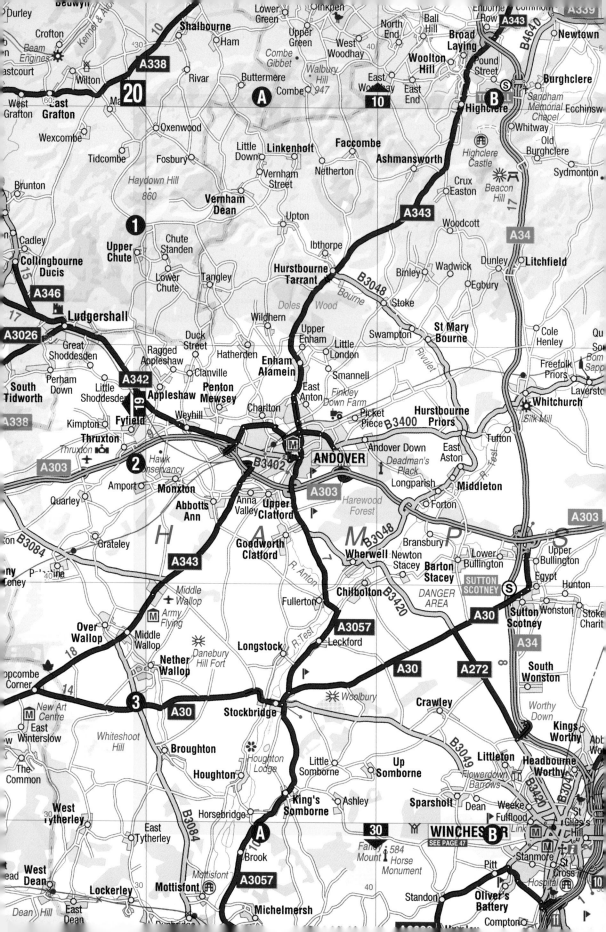

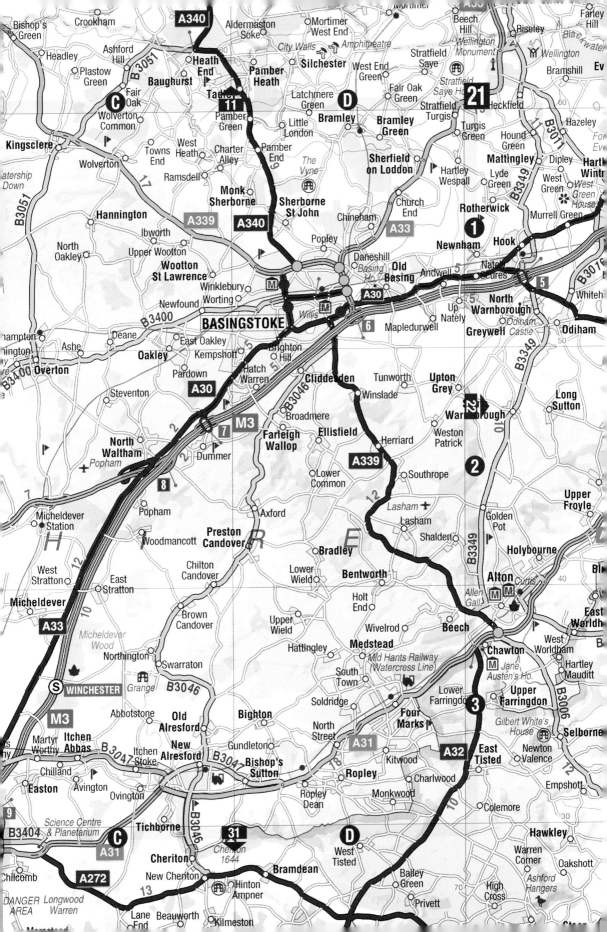

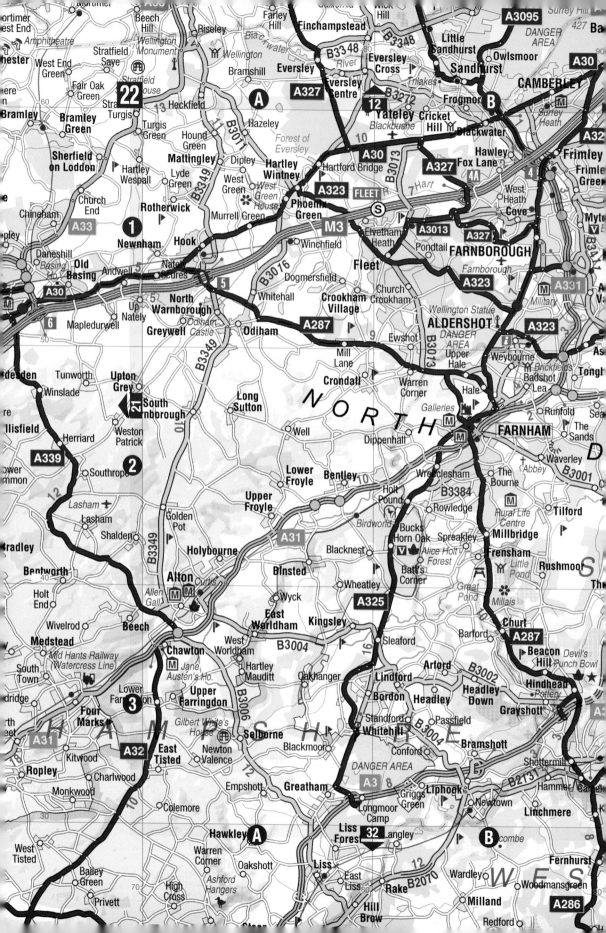

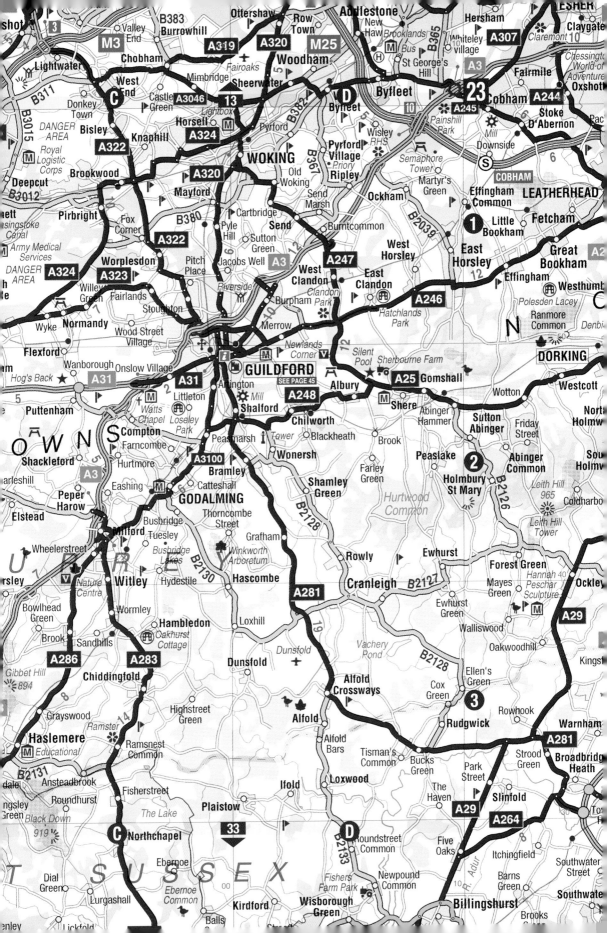

B3224
1290' Rook's Nest
worthy
servoir
Willett
Heathfield
Neck
Courtway
Huntstile
North Petherton
A38

Brompton Ralph
Tolland
Lydeard St Lawrence
Seven Ash
West Bagborough
Terhill
20
Cothelstone
Broomfield
Fyne Court
Shearston
Thurloxton
Adsborough

Clatworthy
30
Tarr
Combe Florey
East Combe
15
Kingston St Mary
Hestercombe
West Monkton

24

Langley Marsh
Whitefield
Ford
Ash Priors
Bishops Lydeard
Fulford
Nailsbourne
Upper Cheddon
Cheddon Fitzpaine
A3259

Langley
Wiveliscombe
Croford
Fitzhead
West Somerset Railway
Gauge
Halse
Cotford St Luke
Langford
Staplegrove
Monkton Heathfield
Creech St Michael

Hartswell
Preston Bowyer
Heathfield
Norton Fitzwarren
Heritage Cen.
Bishop Hull
25
Ruishton
Henlade
Thornfalcon
A358

Milverton
Hillcommon B3227
Oake
A3065
Galmington
TAUNTON
Haydon
Stoke St Mary
Meare Green

Bathealton
Chipley
Houndsmoor
Hillfarrance
Bradford-on-Tone
Rumwell
Trull
SEE PAGE 47
Shoreditch
Orchard Portman
Thurlbear
West Hatch

Stawley
Kittisford
Langford Budville
East Nynehead
A38
Sheppy's Cider
Staplehay
Sellick's Green
Slough Green

Ashbrittle
Appley
Thorne St Margaret
Runnington
Nynehead
Ham
Poole
West Buckland
TAUNTON DEANE
Fulwood
Corfe
Staple Fitzpaine
Blokenh

Cothay Manor
Greenham
Holywell Lake
Tonedale
Payton
Westford
Chelston
Pitminster
Howleigh
Staple Hill
Curland

Holcombe Rogus
Westleigh
Burlescombe
Rockwell Green
WELLINGTON
Angersleigh
Lowton
Blagdon Hill
Curland Common
Blackwater

M5
Ayshford
Appledore
Prescott
Sampford Arundel
Wrangway
Ford Street
918
Resr.
1034
Staple Hill

Nicholashayne
Wellington
BLACKDOWN HILLS
R. Culm
Blindmoor
Buckland St Mary
Ham

TIVERTON
Culmstock
Whitehall
Culm Davy
Clayhidon
Rosemary Lane
Churchstanton
Otterford
Birchwood
Newtown
Street Ash

Uffculme
Northcott
Craddock
845
Castle
Millhayes
Stapley
Royston Water
Bishopswood
Beetham
Northay

Coldharbour Mill
Smithincott
Hackpen Hill
Bolham Water
Churchinford
Marsh
Whitestaunton

Willand
Ashill
Madford
Abbey
Smeatharpe
Howley

Blackborough
Dunkeswell Abbey
Newcott

Kentisbeare
Sheldon
Dunkeswell
Heritage
929
Upottery
Yarcombe
Crawley
A30

Saint Hill
Dunkeswell
Luppitt
Rawridge
14

Dulford
Kerswell
Broadhembury
Chapel
Beacon
A30
Stockland
Furley
Chard

Norman's Green
Colliton
10
Hembury
Wick
Monkton
Millhayes
Membury
Castle

Plymtree
Luton
Upton
Godford Cross
Combe Raleigh
Cotleigh
Heathstock
Turfmoor

Payhembury
Lower Cheriton
Awliscombe
Weston
Lace
Ham
River Yarty
Smallridg

Higher Tale
Colestocks
Higher Cheriton
Buckerell
Wilmington
Dalwood
Loughwood
Church

A30
A Honiton
34
10
Widworthy
Burrow Farm
Axe Valley Wildlife Park
Wey

Talaton
Fenny Bridges
Gittisham
Offwell
B
Shute
Kilmington

Wildwood Escot
Fairmile
Alfington
Church Green
A35
Seaton Junction
Hampton
Abbey

Hand and Pen
Taleford Cadhay
Ottery
Northleigh
Shute Barton
A358

WILLS

M5
24 Huntworth
Westonzoyland
A361
King's Sedge Moor
Butleigh
Barton
St David

Middlezoy
Greylake
Henley
Compton
Dundon 50
West
Lydfo

Pumping
Station
Thorngrove
High
Ham
River Cary
Littleton
B3153
25

Northmoor Green
or Moorland
A361 22
Othery
Beer
Dundon 7
geston
Keinton
Mandeville

North
Newton
C
Pathe
Burrow Mump
Stem
D
Hurcot
B3151

nsel Lock
nal Centre
Bankland
King
Alfred's
A372 15
Bowdens
Low
Ham
Westcombe
Somerton
Charlton
Mackrell
Charlton
Adam

Hedging
V
Burrowbridge
Athelney
Stathe
Aller
DANGER
AREA
Wearne
Pitney
B3153
South
Hill
V
Midney
B3165

West Lyng
East
Lyng
R. Parrett
Wick
R. Tone
Langport
Pict's Hill
1645
Langport
Upton
B3151
Lytes Cary
Manor

field
lton
Meare
Green
Woodhill
Oath
Burton
Pynsent
Curry
Rivel
Portfield
V
Huish
Episcopi
Pibsbury
Long
Sutton
Catsgore
Kingsdon
A303
1 2

North
Curry
Huntham
West Sedge Moor
Drayton
Priest's
House
Muchelney
Knole
8
Northover
B3151
Podimore

Helland
Isle
Abbey
Long
Load
R. Yeo
Ilchester
Yeovilton
M
Air

esdon
Newport 15
A378
B3168
Swell
R. Isle
Muchelney
Ham
Thorney
Milton
Yeovilton
A303
Limingto

Wrantage
Curry
Mallet
Fivehead
Isle
Brewers
Midelney
Town Tree Nature
Stapleton
B3165
15
A303
A37
Draycott

Hatch
auchamp
Hambridge
Lock-up
Kingsbury
Episcopi
Coat
Ash
Tintinhull
Chilthorne
Domer
Yeovil
Marsh

Beercrocombe
RNAS
Merryfield
Westport
Barrington
Court
New
Cross
Stembridge
East
Lambrook
Martock
Treasurer's
House
Tintinhull
M

Hatch Green
A358
Puckington
B3168
West
Lambrook
Mid
Lambrook
Manor
Hurst
Bower
Stoke
sub Hamdon
15
A3088
Preston
Plucknett

Ashill
Ilton
Ilford
Barrington
South
Petherton
Hinton
Priory
East
Stoke
Montacute
26
House
YE

dmill
hill
Rapps
Stocklinch
Shepton
Beauchamp
Moor
A303
Tower
Montacute
Bar

Broadway
Horton
Cross
Winterhay
Green
Whitelackington
Hurcott
Wigborough
Norton sub
Hamdon
Odcombe
Brympton
D'Evercy
2

03
Horton
V
Seavington
St Michael
Over
Stratton
Chiselborough
West
Coker
YE

Donyatt
Ilminster
Kingstone
Seavington
St Mary
Lopen
A356
West
Chinnock
North Coker
East
Coker

Combe St
Nicholas
Sea
Dowlish
Wake
Allowenshay
Dinnington
Hinton
St George
Merriott
Middle
Chinnock
A30
East
Chinnock
Hardington
Moor

Peasmarsh
Knowle
St Giles
Cricket
Malherbie
Chillington
Broadshard
Haselbury
Plucknett
Hardington
Mandeville
Sutton
Bingham

Nimmer
Hornsbury
Cudworth
A30
Roundham
Crewkerne
North
Perrott
Pendomer
Resr

Cuttiford's
Door
Chaffcombe
Lydmarsh
Purtington
Heritage
Centre
M
A3066
Hardington
Marsh
Higher
Halstock Leigh
Halstock
M
Os

Crimchard
M
Lakes &
Gdns.
Hewish
Misterton
South
Perrott
Weston
East
Chelborough

Chard
i
B3162
Street
Cricket St
Thomas
Woolminstone
Wayford
B3165
Chedington
A356
3
West
Chelborough

Burridge
Forton
Whatley
Winsham
Clapton
Seaborough
Corscombe
Benville

Tatworth
B3167
Perry
Street
Bridge
Horn
Ash
Drimpton
Littlewindsor
Mosterton
A3066
Dibberford
Higher

stock
South
Chard
Forde
Abbey
Laymore
Greenham
B3164
A3066
Newtown
A356
Rampis

A358
Tytherleigh
Holditch
Hewood
Thorncombe
Blackdown
Burstock
Hursey
B3163
Beaminster
M
B3163
Toller
Whelme
Up

chillo
ston
South
Common
Lower
Holditch
Birdsmoorgate
Pilsdon Pen
Broadwindsor
B3164
Stoke
Abbott
13
Mapperton
Hooke
Higher
K combe

croft
Hawkchurch
C
B3165
Marshalsea
Bettiscombe
Ilsdon
Blackney
North
ood
Netherbury
Mapperton
North
Poorton
Lower
Kingcombe

Axminster
Blackpool
Corner
Lambert's
Castle
35
Marsh
ood
Monkwood
South
Bowood
D
Loscombe
South
Poorton
T
Po

B3261
Raymond's
Hill
Monkton
Wyld
Coney's
Castle
Fishpond
Bottom
R. Char
Marshwood Vale
Filford
B3162
Waytown
Oxbridge
Salway Ash
West
Milton
Powerstock

Wootton
Fitzpaine
Whitchurch
A3066

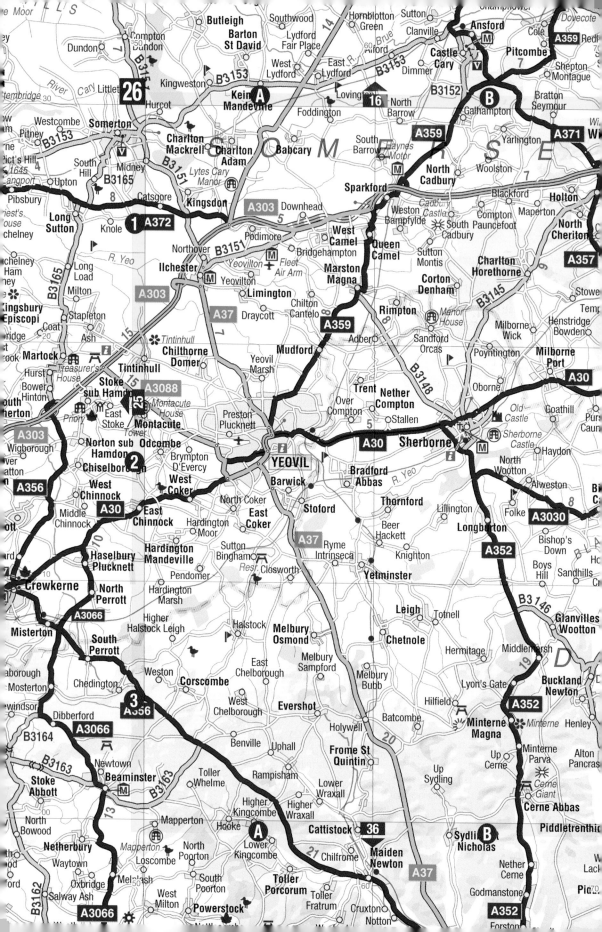

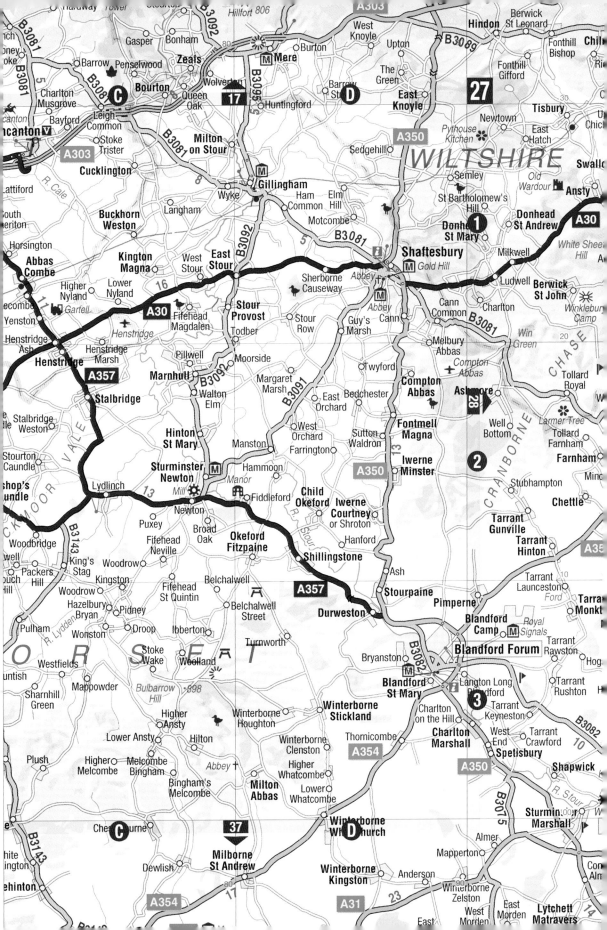

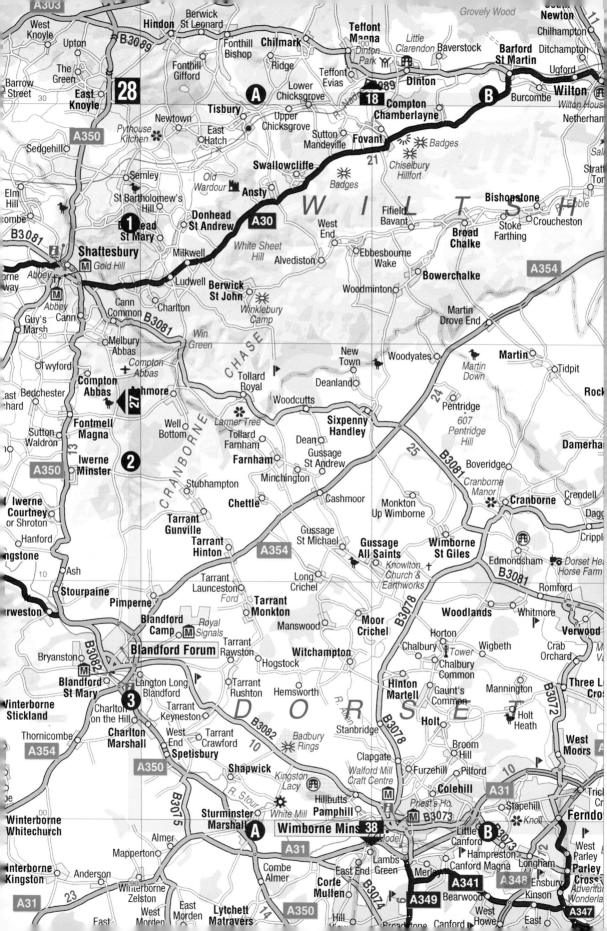

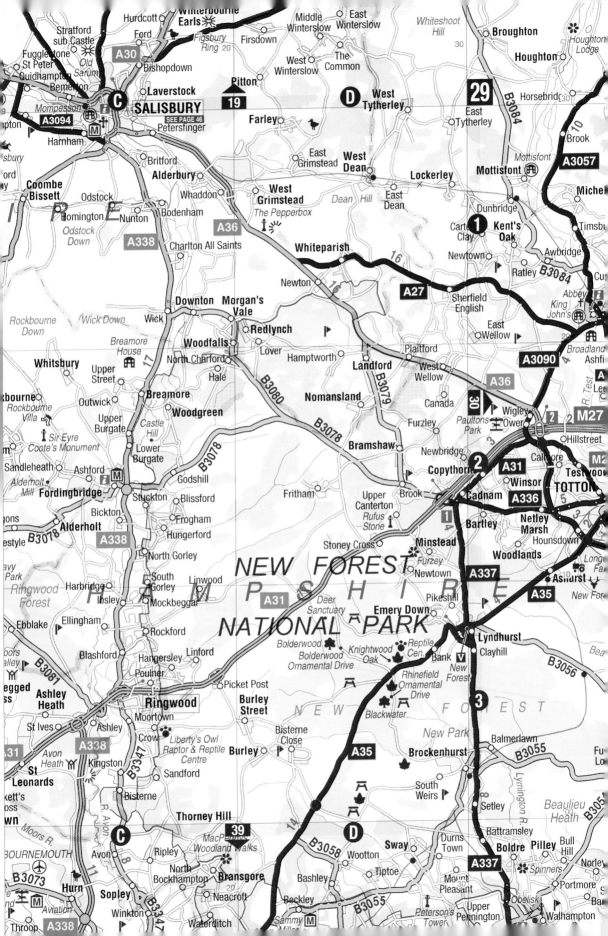

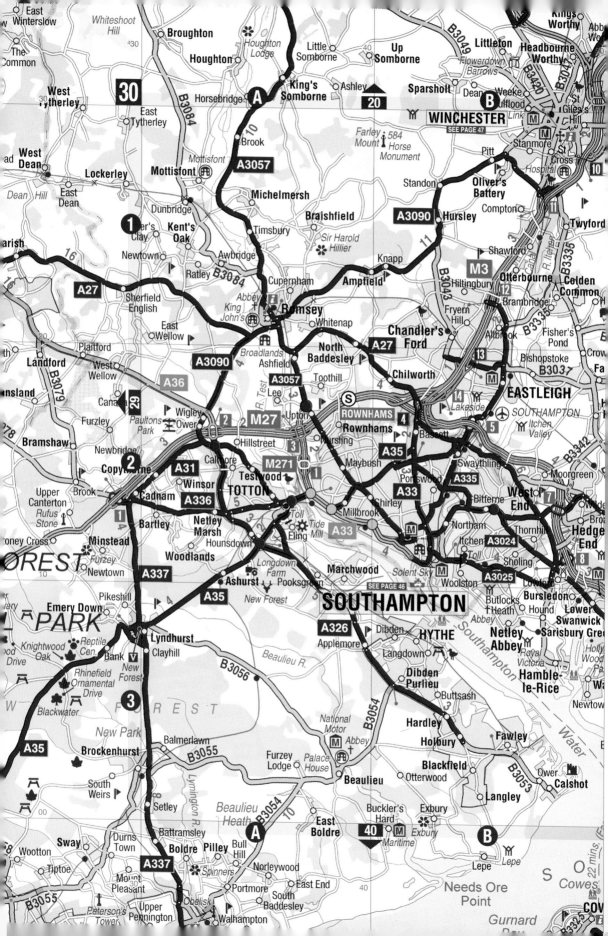

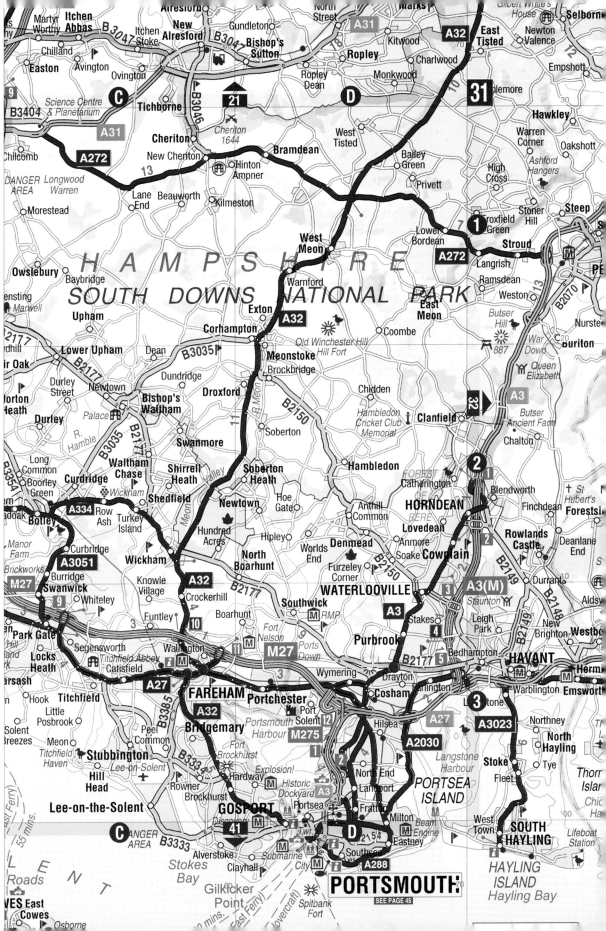

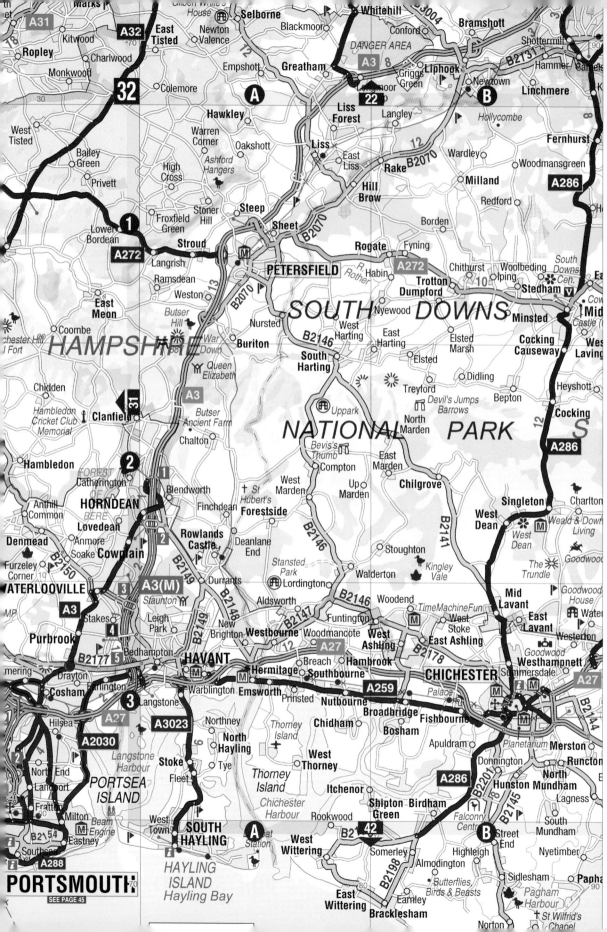

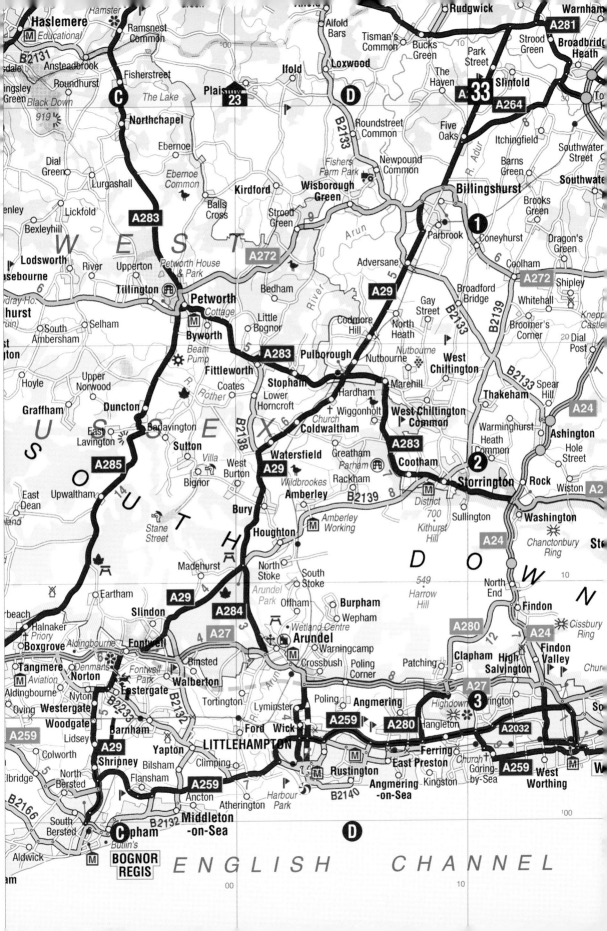

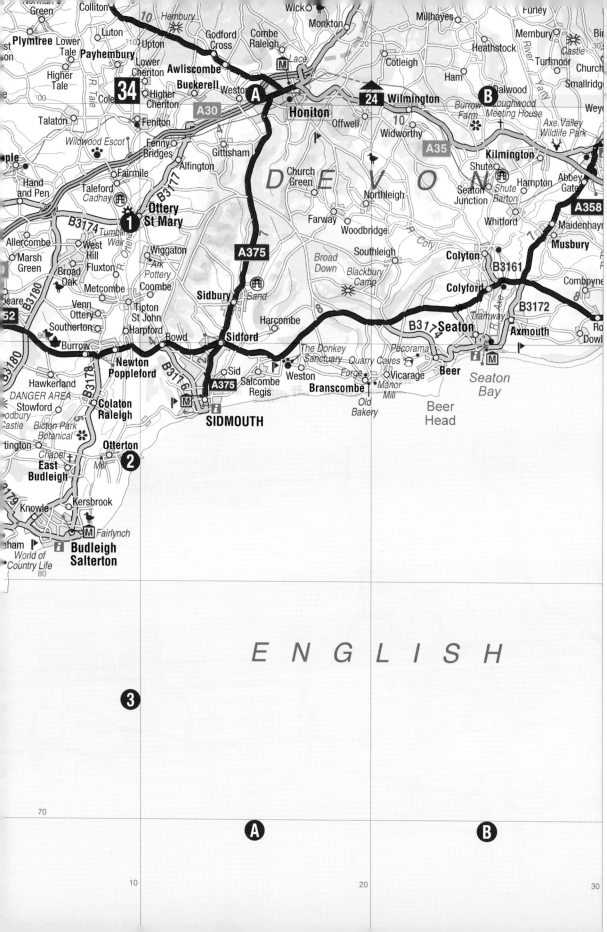

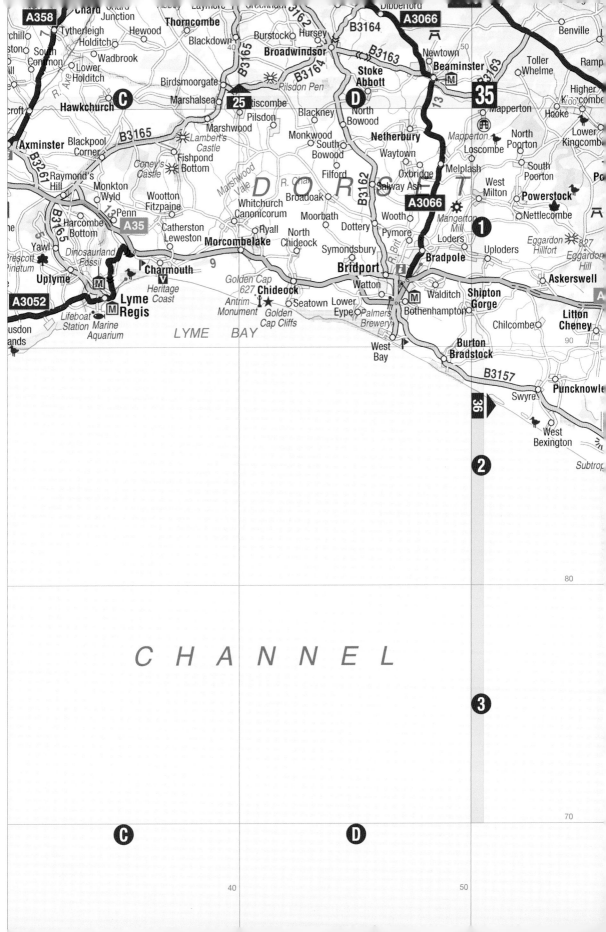

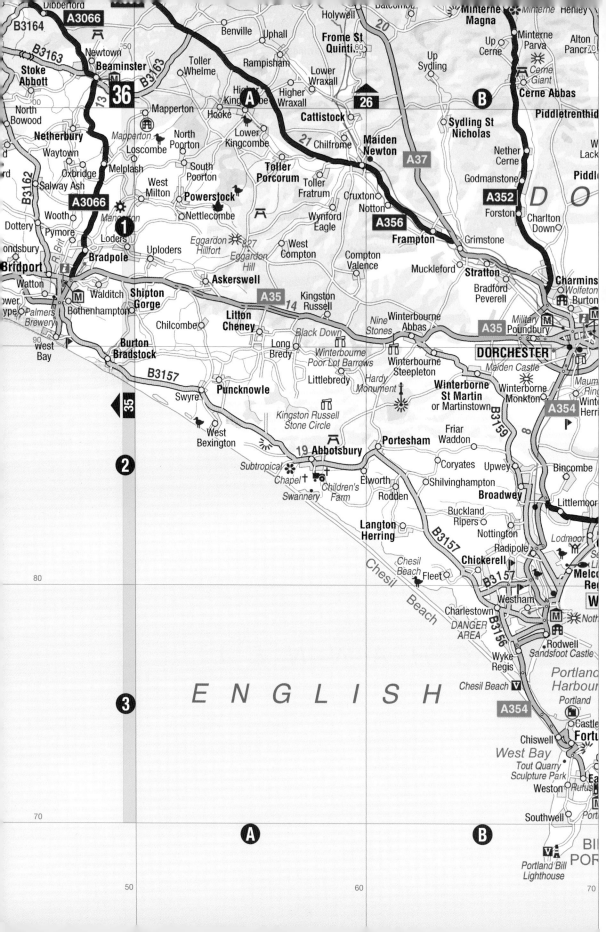

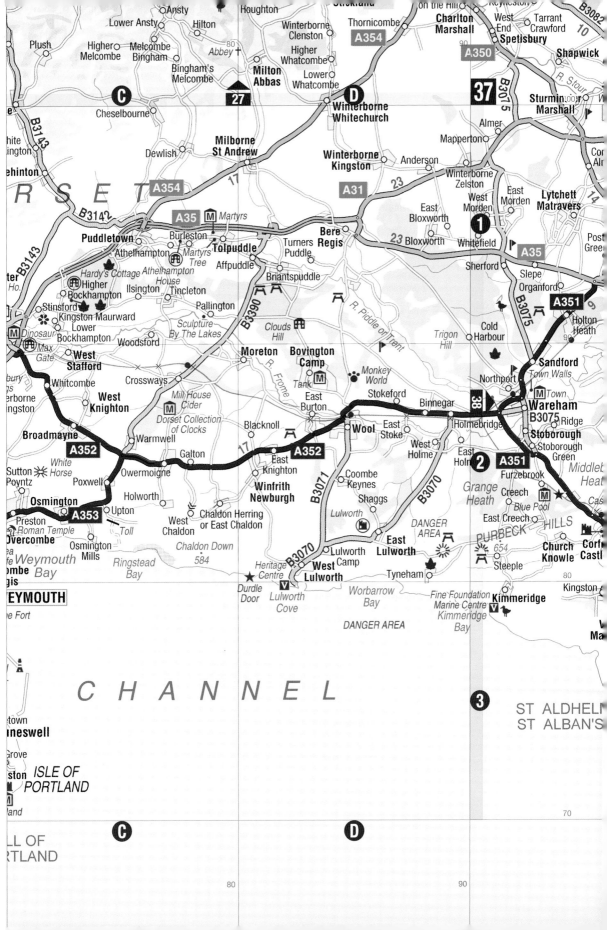

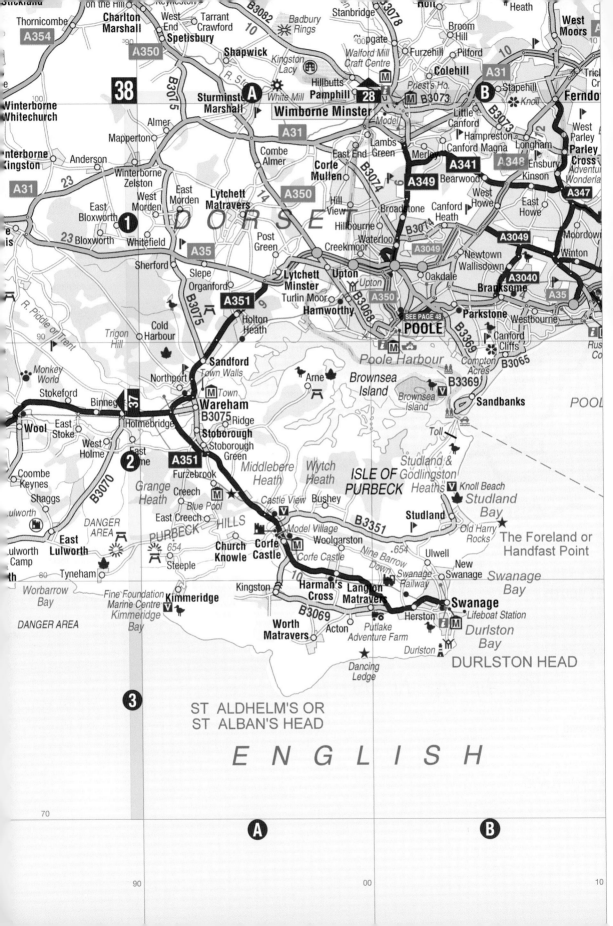

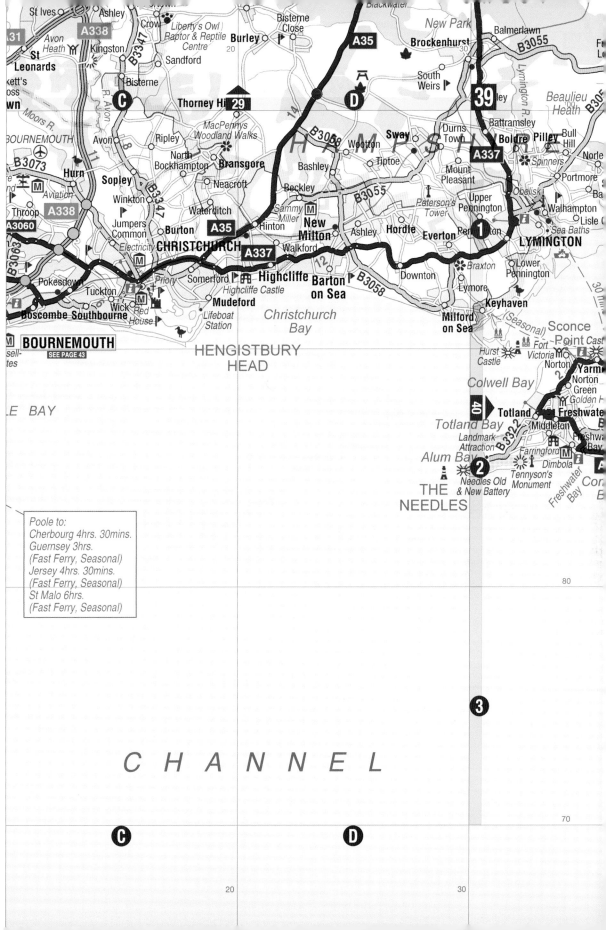

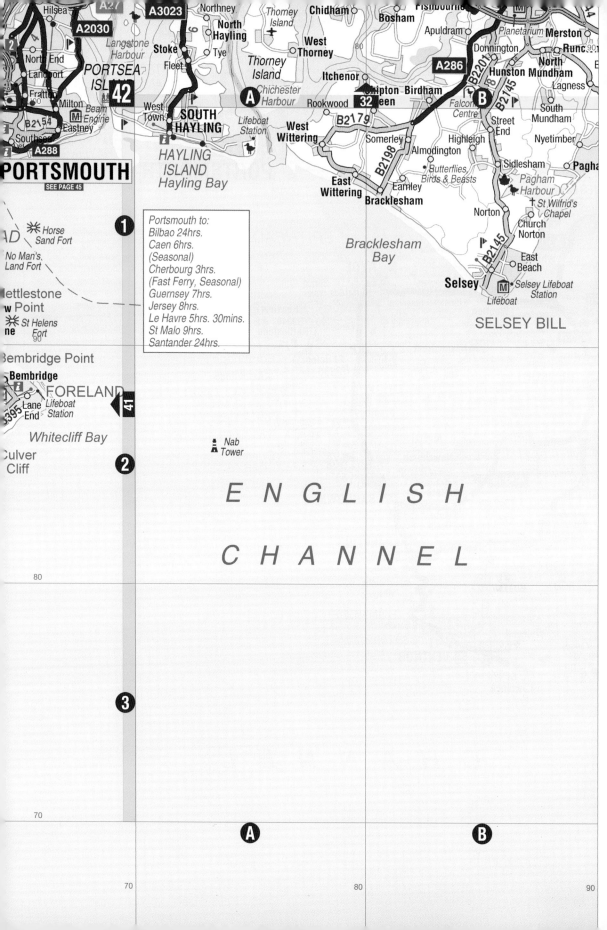

CITY & TOWN CENTRE PLANS

Bath	43	Portsmouth	45	Taunton	47
Bournemouth	43	Reading	46	Winchester	47
Bristol	44	Salisbury	46	Windsor	47
Cardiff	44	Southampton	46	London Heathrow Airport	48
Guildford	45	Swindon	47	Poole Port Plan	48

Reference to Town Plans

Motorway	**M3**	Abbey, Cathedral, Priory etc.	✝
Motorway Under Construction		Bus Station	●
Motorway Junctions with Numbers	**4** **5**	Car Park (Selection of)	P
Unlimited Interchange **4** Limited Interchange **5**		Church	✝
		City Wall	ᴖᴖᴖᴖᴖ
Primary Route	**A33**	Ferry (vehicular) ⛴ (foot only)	
Dual Carriageways	**A30**	Golf Course	
Class A Road	**B2070**	Heliport	Ⓗ
Class B Road		Hospital	Ⓗ
Major Roads Under Construction		Lighthouse	
Major Roads Proposed		Market	
Minor Roads		National Trust Property (open)	NT
Fuel Station		(restricted opening)	NT
Restricted Access		Park & Ride	P+R
Pedestrianized Road & Main Footway		Place of Interest	■
One Way Streets	→ →	Police Station	▲
Toll	Toll	Post Office	★
Railway and Station		Shopping Area (Main street and precinct)	
Underground / Metro & D.L.R. Station	DLR	Shopmobility	
Level Crossing and Tunnel		Toilet	▽
Tram Stop and One Way Tram Stop		Tourist Information Centre	i
Built-up Area		Viewpoint	☀
		Visitor Information Centre	V

BATH

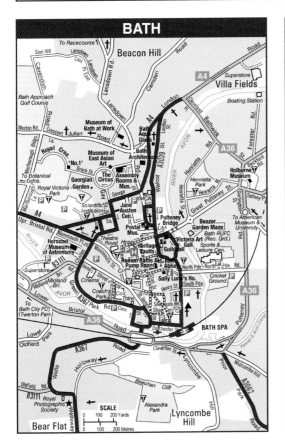

BOURNEMOUTH

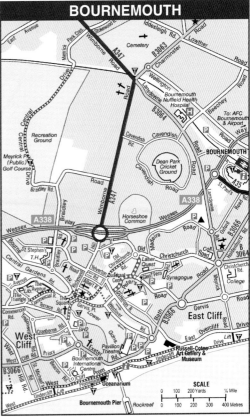

BRISTOL

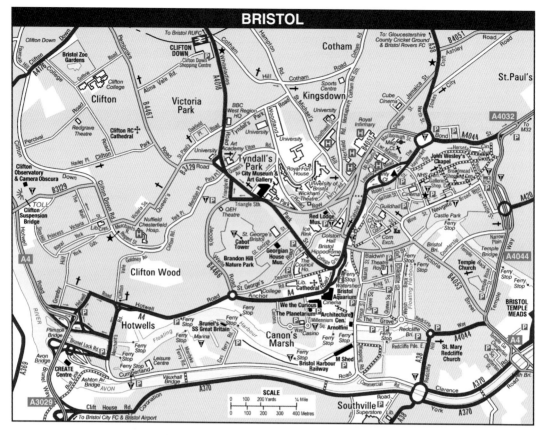

CARDIFF (CAERDYDD)

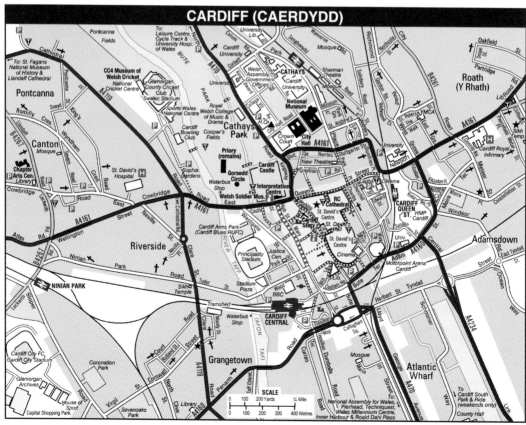

GUILDFORD

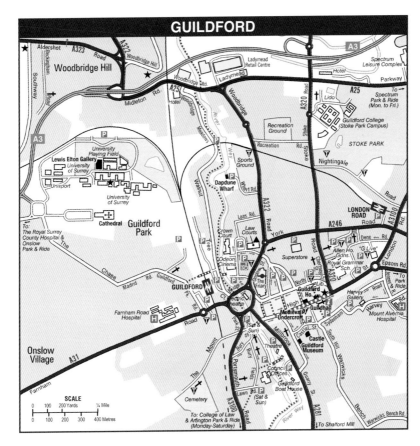

PORTSMOUTH

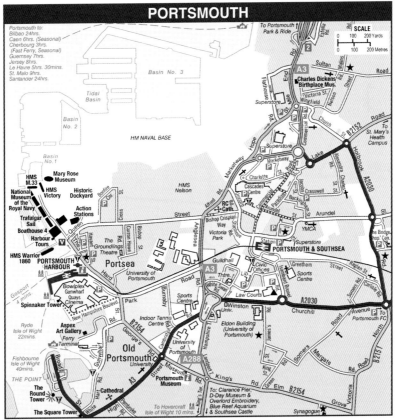

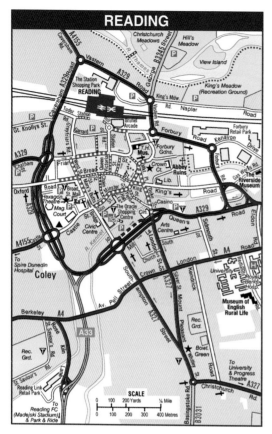

READING

SALISBURY

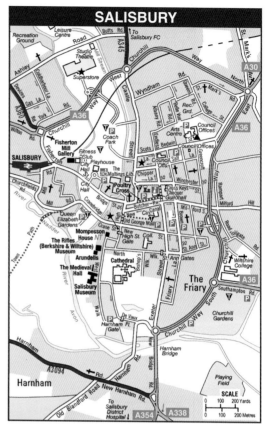

SOUTHAMPTON

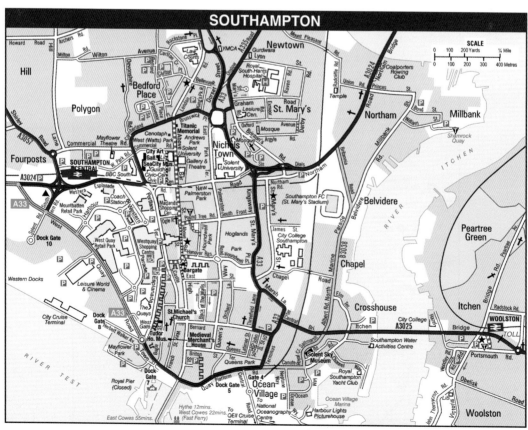

46 Southern England Regional Atlas

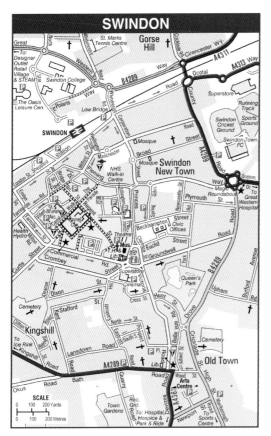

SWINDON

TAUNTON

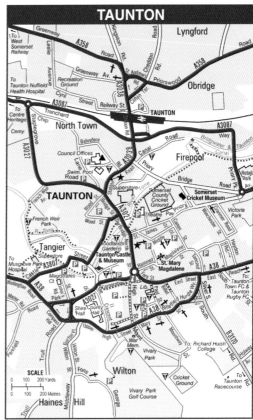

WINCHESTER

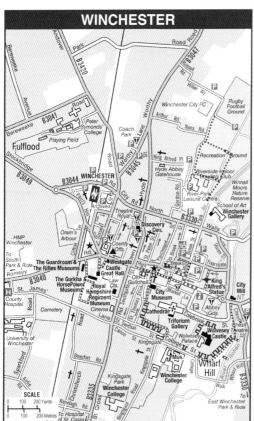

WINDSOR

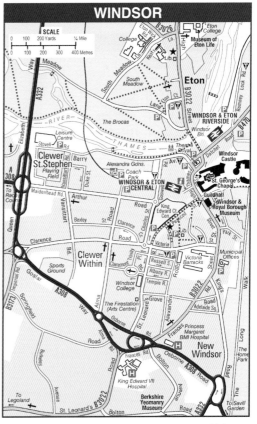

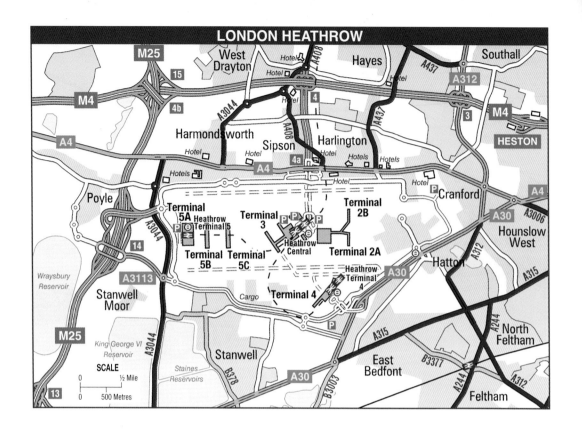

LONDON HEATHROW

West Drayton · Hayes · Southall · Harmondsworth · Sipson · Harlington · HESTON · Poyle · Cranford · Stanwell Moor · Hounslow West · Hatton · Stanwell · North Feltham · East Bedfont · Feltham

Terminal 5A · Heathrow Terminal 5 · Terminal 3 · Terminal 2B · Terminal 5B · Terminal 5C · Heathrow Central · Terminal 2A · Terminal 4 · Heathrow Terminal 4 · Cargo

Wraybury Reservoir · King George VI Reservoir · Staines Reservoirs

M25 · M4 · A4 · A3044 · A408 · A437 · A312 · A30 · A3006 · A315 · A312 · A244 · B3377 · B378 · B3003 · A3113 · A3044

SCALE
0 — ½ Mile
0 — 500 Metres

POOLE

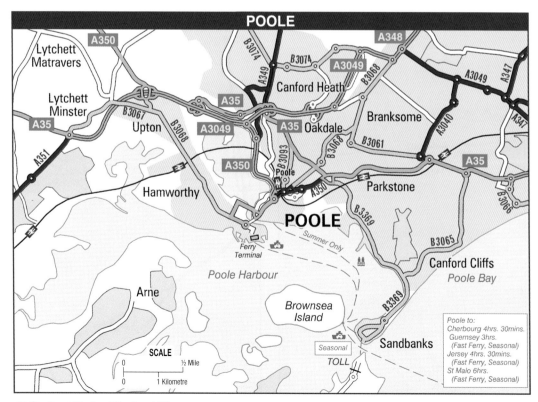

Lytchett Matravers · Lytchett Minster · Canford Heath · Branksome · Upton · Oakdale · Hamworthy · Poole · Parkstone · POOLE · Arne · Canford Cliffs · Poole Bay · Brownsea Island · Sandbanks

Poole Harbour · Ferry Terminal · Summer Only · Seasonal · TOLL

A350 · A348 · B3074 · B3074 · A349 · B3049 · A3049 · A347 · A35 · B3067 · B3068 · A3049 · A35 · B3061 · B3040 · A347 · A351 · A350 · B3093 · B3068 · B3369 · B3065 · B3369 · B3066

Poole to:
Cherbourg 4hrs. 30mins.
Guernsey 3hrs.
 (Fast Ferry, Seasonal)
Jersey 4hrs. 30mins.
 (Fast Ferry, Seasonal)
St Malo 6hrs.
 (Fast Ferry, Seasonal)

SCALE
0 — ½ Mile
0 — 1 Kilometre

48 Southern England Regional Atlas

1. A strict alphabetical order is used e.g. Bishop Sutton follows Bishopstrow but precedes Bishop's Waltham.

2. The map reference given refers to the actual map square in which the town spot or built-up area is located and not to the place name.

3. Only one reference is given although due to page overlaps the place may appear on more than one page.

4. Where two or more places of the same name occur in the same County or Unitary Authority, the nearest large town is also given; e.g. Allington *Wilts*.....3D **19** (nr Amesbury) indicates that Allington is located in square 3D on page **19** and is situated near Amesbury in the County of Wiltshire.

5. Major towns & destinations are shown in bold i.e. **Bath** *Bath*.....**43** (3C **7**). Where they appear on a Town Plan a second page reference is given.

COUNTIES AND UNITARY AUTHORITIES with the abbreviations used in this index

Bath & N E Somerset : *Bath*
Bournemouth : *Bour*
Bracknell Forest : *Brac*
Bristol : *Bris*
Buckinghamshire : *Buck*
Caerphilly : *Cphy*
Cardiff : *Card*
Devon : *Devn*
Dorset : *Dors*

Gloucestershire : *Glos*
Greater London : *G Lon*
Hampshire : *Hants*
Hertfordshire : *Herts*
Isle of Wight : *IOW*
Monmouthshire : *Mon*
Newport : *Newp*
North Somerset : *N Som*
Oxfordshire : *Oxon*

Poole : *Pool*
Portsmouth : *Port*
Reading : *Read*
Rhondda Cynon Taff : *Rhon*
Slough : *Slo*
Somerset : *Som*
South Gloucestershire : *S Glo*
Southampton : *Sotn*
Surrey : *Surr*

Swindon : *Swin*
Torfaen : *Torf*
Vale of Glamorgan : *V Glam*
West Berkshire : *W Ber*
West Sussex : *W Sus*
Wiltshire : *Wilts*
Windsor & Maidenhead : *Wind*
Wokingham : *Wok*

INDEX

A

Abbas Combe *Som*	1C **27**
Abbey *Devn*	2A **24**
Abbey Gate *Devn*	1B **34**
Abbotsbury *Dors*	2A **36**
Abbots Leigh *N Som*	2A **6**
Abbotstone *Hants*	3C **21**
Abbots Worthy *Hants*	3B **20**
Abbotts Ann *Hants*	2A **20**
Abertridwr *Cphy*	1A **4**
Abinger Common *Surr*	2D **23**
Abinger Hammer *Surr*	2D **23**
Ablington *Wilts*	2C **19**
Abson *S Glo*	2C **7**
Acton *Dors*	3A **38**
Acton Turville *S Glo*	1D **7**
Adber *Dors*	1B **26**
Addlestone *Surr*	3D **13**
Adgestone *IOW*	2C **41**
Adsborough *Som*	1B **24**
Adversane *W Sus*	1D **33**
Affpuddle *Dors*	1D **37**
Aisholt *Som*	3A **14**
Albury *Surr*	2D **23**
Aldbourne *Wilts*	2D **9**
Alderbury *Wilts*	1C **29**
Alderholt *Dors*	2C **29**
Alderley *Glos*	1C **7**
Aldermaston *W Ber*	3C **11**
Aldermaston Soke *Hants*	3D **11**
Aldermaston Wharf *W Ber*	3D **11**
Aldershot *Hants*	1B **22**
Alderton *Wilts*	1D **7**
Aldingbourne *W Sus*	3C **33**
Aldsworth *W Sus*	3A **32**
Aldwick *W Sus*	3C **33**
Aldworth *W Ber*	2C **11**
Aley *Som*	3A **14**
Alfington *Devn*	1A **34**
Alfold *Surr*	3D **23**
Alfold Bars *W Sus*	3D **23**
Alfold Crossways *Surr*	3D **23**
Alford *Som*	3B **16**
Alhampton *Som*	3B **16**
Allbrook *Hants*	1B **30**
All Cannings *Wilts*	3B **8**
Aller *Som*	1D **25**
Allercombe *Devn*	1A **34**
Allington *Wilts*	3D **19**
	(nr Amesbury)
Allington *Wilts*	3B **8**
	(nr Devizes)
Allowenshay *Som*	2C **25**
Almer *Dors*	1A **38**
Almodington *W Sus*	1B **42**
Almondsbury *S Glo*	1B **6**
Alston *Devn*	3C **25**
Alstone *Som*	2C **15**
Alston Sutton *Som*	1D **15**
Alton *Hants*	3A **22**
Alton Barnes *Wilts*	3C **9**
Alton Pancras *Dors*	3C **27**
Alton Priors *Wilts*	3C **9**
Alvediston *Wilts*	1A **28**
Alverstoke *Hants*	1C **41**
Alverstone *IOW*	2C **41**
Alveston *S Glo*	1B **6**
Alweston *Dors*	2B **26**

Amberley *W Sus*	2D **33**
Amesbury *Wilts*	2C **19**
Ampfield *Hants*	1A **30**
Amport *Hants*	2D **19**
Ancton *W Sus*	3C **33**
Anderson *Dors*	1D **37**
Andover *Hants*	2A **20**
Andover Down *Hants*	2A **20**
Andwell *Hants*	1D **21**
Angersleigh *Som*	2A **24**
Angmering *W Sus*	3D **33**
Angmering-on-Sea *W Sus*	3D **33**
Anmore *Hants*	2D **31**
Anna Valley *Hants*	2A **20**
Ansford *Som*	3B **16**
Ansteadbrook *Surr*	3C **23**
Ansty *Wilts*	1A **28**
Anthill Common *Hants*	2D **31**
Appledore *Devn*	2A **24**
Appleford *Oxon*	1C **11**
Applemore *Hants*	3A **30**
Appleshaw *Hants*	2A **20**
Appley *Som*	1A **24**
Apse Heath *IOW*	2C **41**
Apuldram *W Sus*	3B **32**
Arborfield *Wok*	3A **12**
Arborfield Cross *Wok*	3A **12**
Arborfield Garrison *Wok*	3A **12**
Ardington *Oxon*	1B **10**
Arford *Hants*	3B **22**
Arne *Dors*	2A **38**
Arreton *IOW*	2C **41**
Artington *Surr*	2C **23**
Arundel *W Sus*	3D **33**
Ascot *Wind*	3C **13**
Ash *Dors*	2D **27**
Ash *Som*	1D **25**
Ash *Surr*	1B **22**
Ashampstead *W Ber*	2C **11**
Ashbrittle *Som*	1A **24**
Ashbury *Oxon*	1D **9**
Ashcott *Som*	3D **15**
Ashe *Hants*	2C **21**
Ashey *IOW*	2C **41**
Ashfield *Hants*	2A **30**
Ashford *Hants*	2C **29**
Ashford *Surr*	2D **13**
Ashford Hill *Hants*	3C **11**
Ashill *Som*	2C **25**
Ashill *Devn*	2A **24**
Ashington *W Sus*	2D **33**
Ashley *Hants*	1D **39**
	(nr New Milton)
Ashley *Hants*	3A **30**
	(nr Winchester)
Ashley *Dors*	3C **29**
Ashley *Wilts*	3D **7**
Ashley Heath *Dors*	3C **29**
Ashmansworth *Hants*	1B **20**
Ashmore *Dors*	2A **28**
Ashmore Green *W Ber*	3C **11**
Ash Priors *Som*	1A **24**
Ashton Common *Wilts*	1D **17**
Ashurst *Hants*	2A **30**
Ash Vale *Surr*	1B **22**
Ashwick *Som*	2B **16**
Askerswell *Dors*	1A **36**
Aston *Wok*	1A **12**
Aston Tirrold *Oxon*	1C **11**

Aston Upthorpe *Oxon*	1C **11**
Athelhampton *Dors*	1C **37**
Athelney *Som*	1C **25**
Atherfield Green *IOW*	3B **40**
Atherington *W Sus*	3D **33**
Atworth *Wilts*	3D **7**
Aughton *Wilts*	1D **19**
Aust *S Glo*	1A **6**
Avebury *Wilts*	3C **9**
Avebury Trusloe *Wilts*	3B **8**
Avington *Hants*	3C **21**
Avon *Hants*	1C **39**
Avonmouth *Bris*	2A **6**
Awbridge *Hants*	1A **30**
Awliscombe *Devn*	3A **24**
Axbridge *Som*	1D **15**
Axford *Hants*	2D **21**
Axford *Wilts*	3D **9**
Axminster *Devn*	1C **35**
Axmouth *Devn*	1B **34**
Ayshford *Devn*	2A **24**

B

Babcary *Som*	1A **26**
Backwell *N Som*	3D **5**
Badbury *Swin*	1C **9**
Badgworth *Som*	1C **15**
Badminton *S Glo*	1D **7**
Badshot Lea *Surr*	2B **22**
Bagley *Som*	2D **15**
Bagnor *W Ber*	3B **10**
Bagshot *Surr*	3C **13**
Bagshot *Wilts*	3A **10**
Bagstone *S Glo*	1B **6**
Bailey Green *Hants*	1D **31**
Ball Hill *Hants*	3B **10**
Balls Cross *W Sus*	1C **33**
Balmerlawn *Hants*	3A **30**
Baltonsborough *Som*	3A **16**
Bank *Hants*	3D **29**
Bankland *Som*	1C **25**
Banwell *N Som*	1C **15**
Bapton *Wilts*	3A **18**
Barford *Hants*	3B **22**
Barford St Martin *Wilts*	3B **18**
Barkham *Wok*	3A **12**
Barlavington *W Sus*	2C **33**
Barnham *W Sus*	3C **33**
Barns Green *W Sus*	1D **33**
Barri *V Glam*	3A **4**
Barrington *Som*	2C **25**
Barrow *Som*	3C **17**
Barrow Common *Som*	3A **6**
Barrow Gurney *N Som*	3A **6**
Barrow Street *Wilts*	3D **17**
Barry *V Glam*	3A **4**
Barry Island *V Glam*	3A **4**
Bartley *Hants*	2A **30**
Barton *IOW*	2C **41**
Barton *N Som*	1C **15**
Barton on Sea *Hants*	1D **39**
Barton St David *Som*	3A **16**
Barton Stacey *Hants*	2B **20**
Barwick *Som*	2A **26**
Bashley *Hants*	1D **39**
Basingstoke *Hants*	1D **21**
Bason Bridge *Som*	2C **15**
Bassaleg *Newp*	1B **4**

Bassett *Sotn*	2B **30**
Batchworth *Herts*	1D **13**
Batcombe *Dors*	3B **26**
Batcombe *Som*	3B **16**
Bath *Bath*	**43** (3C **7**)
Bathampton *Bath*	3C **7**
Bathealton *Som*	1A **24**
Batheaston *Bath*	3C **7**
Bathford *Bath*	3C **7**
Bathpool *Som*	1B **24**
Bathway *Som*	1A **16**
Battleborough *Som*	1C **15**
Battramsley *Hants*	1A **40**
Batt's Corner *Surr*	2B **22**
Baughurst *Hants*	3C **11**
Baulking *Oxon*	1A **10**
Baverstock *Wilts*	3B **18**
Bawdrip *Som*	3C **15**
Baybridge *Hants*	1C **31**
Baydon *Wilts*	2D **9**
Bayford *Som*	1C **27**
Beach *S Glo*	2C **7**
Beachley *Glos*	1A **6**
Beacon *Devn*	3A **24**
Beacon Hill *Surr*	3B **22**
Beaconsfield *Buck*	1C **13**
Beaminster *Dors*	3D **25**
Beanacre *Wilts*	3A **8**
Bearwood *Pool*	1B **38**
Beaulieu *Hants*	3A **30**
Beauworth *Hants*	1C **31**
Beckhampton *Wilts*	3B **8**
Beckington *Som*	1D **17**
Beckley *Hants*	1D **39**
Bedchester *Dors*	2D **27**
Beddau *Rhon*	1A **4**
Bedham *W Sus*	1D **33**
Bedhampton *Hants*	3A **32**
Bedminster *Bris*	2A **6**
Bedwas *Cphy*	1A **4**
Beech *Hants*	3D **21**
Beech Hill *W Ber*	3D **11**
Beechingstoke *Wilts*	1B **18**
Beedon *W Ber*	2B **10**
Beenham *W Ber*	3C **11**
Beer *Devn*	2B **34**
Beer *Som*	3D **15**
Beercrocombe *Som*	1C **25**
Beer Hackett *Dors*	2B **26**
Beetham *Som*	2B **24**
Began *Card*	1B **4**
Beggearn Huish *Som*	3A **14**
Belchalwell *Dors*	3C **27**
Belchalwell Street *Dors*	3C **27**
Bembridge *IOW*	2D **41**
Bemerton *Wilts*	3C **19**
Benson *Oxon*	1D **11**
Bentley *Hants*	2A **22**
Bentworth *Hants*	2D **21**
Benville *Dors*	3A **26**
Bepton *W Sus*	2B **32**
Bere Regis *Dors*	1D **37**
Berkley *Som*	2D **17**
Berrick Salome *Oxon*	1D **11**
Berrow *Som*	1C **15**
Berwick Bassett *Wilts*	2C **9**
Berwick St James *Wilts*	3B **18**
Berwick St John *Wilts*	1A **28**
Berwick St Leonard *Wilts*	3A **18**

Bettiscombe Dors ...1D **35**
Bettws Newp ...1B **4**
Beverston Glos ...1D **7**
Bexleyhill W Sus ...1C **33**
Bickenhall Som ...2B **24**
Bicknoller Som ...3A **14**
Bickton Hants ...2C **29**
Biddestone Wilts ...2D **7**
Biddisham Som ...1C **15**
Bierley IOW ...3C **41**
Bighton Hants ...3D **21**
Bignor W Sus ...2C **33**
Billingshurst W Sus ...1D **33**
Bilsham W Sus ...3C **33**
Bincombe Dors ...2B **36**
Binegar Som ...2B **16**
Binfield Brac ...2B **12**
Binfield Heath Oxon ...2A **12**
Bingham's Melcombe Dors ...3C **27**
Binley Hants ...1B **20**
Binnegar Dors ...2D **37**
Binstead IOW ...1C **41**
Binsted Hants ...2A **22**
Binsted W Sus ...3C **33**
Birchgrove Card ...1A **4**
Birchill Devn ...3C **25**
Birchwood Som ...2B **24**
Birdham W Sus ...3B **32**
Birdsmoorgate Dors ...3C **25**
Bisham Wind ...1B **12**
Bishopdown Wilts ...3C **19**
Bishops Cannings Wilts ...3B **8**
Bishop's Caundle Dors ...2B **26**
Bishop's Down Dors ...2B **26**
Bishop's Green Hants ...3C **11**
Bishop's Hull Som ...1B **24**
Bishops Lydeard Som ...1A **24**
Bishop's Sutton Hants ...3D **21**
Bishopstoke Hants ...2B **30**
Bishopstone Swin ...1D **9**
Bishopstone Wilts ...1B **28**
Bishopstrow Wilts ...2D **17**
Bishop Sutton Bath ...1A **16**
Bishop's Waltham Hants ...2C **31**
Bishopswood Som ...2B **24**
Bishopsworth Bris ...3A **6**
Bishton Newp ...1C **5**
Bisley Surr ...1C **23**
Bisterne Hants ...3C **29**
Bisterne Close Hants ...3D **29**
Bitterne Sotn ...2B **30**
Bitton S Glo ...3B **6**
Bix Oxon ...1A **12**
Blackborough Devn ...3A **24**
Blackdown Dors ...3C **25**
Blackfield Hants ...3B **30**
Blackford Som ...2D **15**
...(nr Burnham-on-Sea)
Blackford Som ...1B **26**
...(nr Wincanton)
Blackgang IOW ...3B **40**
Blackheath Surr ...2D **23**
Blackland Wilts ...3B **8**
Blackmoor Hants ...3A **22**
Blacknest Hants ...2A **22**
Blackney Dors ...1D **35**
Blacknoll Dors ...2D **37**
Blackpool Corner Dors ...1C **35**
Blacktown Newp ...1B **4**
Blackwater Som ...2B **24**
Blackwater Hants ...1B **22**
Blackwater IOW ...2C **41**
Blagdon N Som ...1A **16**
Blagdon Hill Som ...2B **24**
Blandford Camp Dors ...3A **28**
Blandford Forum Dors ...3D **27**
Blandford St Mary Dors ...3D **27**
Blashford Hants ...3C **29**
Blatchbridge Som ...2C **17**
Bleadney Som ...2D **15**
Bleadon N Som ...1C **15**
Blendworth Hants ...2A **32**
Blewbury Oxon ...1C **11**
Blindmoor Som ...2B **24**
Blissford Hants ...2C **29**
Bloxworth Dors ...1D **37**
Blunsdon St Andrew Swin ...1C **9**
Boarhunt Hants ...3D **31**
Bodenham Wilts ...1C **29**
Bognor Regis W Sus ...3C **33**
Boldre Hants ...1A **40**
Bolham Water Devn ...2A **24**
Bonchurch IOW ...3C **41**
Bonham Wilts ...3C **17**
Bonvilston V Glam ...2A **4**
Booker Buck ...1B **12**
Boorley Green Hants ...2C **31**

Borden W Sus ...1B **32**
Bordon Hants ...3A **22**
Boreham Wilts ...2D **17**
Boscombe Bour ...1C **39**
Boscombe Wilts ...3D **19**
Bosham W Sus ...3B **32**
Bothampstead W Ber ...2C **11**
Bothenhampton Dors ...1D **35**
Botley Hants ...2C **31**
Bottlesford Wilts ...1C **19**
Bouldnor IOW ...2A **40**
Bourne, The Surr ...2B **22**
Bourne End Buck ...1B **12**
Bournemouth Bour ...**43** (1B **38**)
Bournemouth Airport Dors ...1C **39**
Bourton Dors ...3C **17**
Bourton N Som ...3C **5**
Bourton Oxon ...1D **9**
Bourville Wilts ...3B **8**
Boveney Buck ...2C **13**
Boveridge Dors ...2B **28**
Bovingdon Green Buck ...1B **12**
Bovington Camp Dors ...2D **37**
Bowcombe IOW ...2B **40**
Bowd Devn ...2A **34**
Bowden Hill Wilts ...3A **8**
Bowdens Som ...1D **25**
Bowerchalke Wilts ...1B **28**
Bowerhill Wilts ...3A **8**
Bower Hinton Som ...2D **25**
Bowlhead Green Surr ...3C **23**
Bowlish Som ...2B **16**
Box Wilts ...3D **7**
Boxford W Ber ...2B **10**
Boxgrove W Sus ...3C **33**
Box Hill Wilts ...3D **7**
Boys Hill Dors ...2B **26**
Boyton Wilts ...3A **18**
Bracklesham W Sus ...1B **42**
Bracknell Brac ...3B **12**
Bradenstoke Wilts ...2B **8**
Bradfield W Ber ...2D **11**
Bradford Abbas Dors ...2A **26**
Bradford Leigh Wilts ...3D **7**
Bradford-on-Avon Wilts ...3D **7**
Bradford-on-Tone Som ...1A **24**
Bradford Peverell Dors ...1B **36**
Brading IOW ...2D **41**
Bradley Glos ...1C **7**
Bradley Hants ...2D **21**
Bradley Cross Som ...1D **15**
Bradley Green Som ...3B **14**
Bradley Stoke S Glo ...1B **6**
Bradpole Dors ...1D **35**
Braishfield Hants ...1A **30**
Brambridge Hants ...1B **30**
Bramdean Hants ...1D **31**
Bramley Hants ...1D **21**
Bramley Surr ...2D **23**
Bramley Green Hants ...1D **21**
Bramshaw Hants ...2D **29**
Bramshill Hants ...3A **12**
Bramshott Hants ...3A **22**
Branksome Pool ...1B **38**
Bransbury Hants ...2B **20**
Branscombe Devn ...2A **34**
Bransgore Hants ...1C **39**
Branstone IOW ...2C **41**
Bratton Wilts ...1A **18**
Bratton Seymour Som ...1B **26**
Bray Wind ...2C **13**
Bray Wick Wind ...2B **12**
Breach W Sus ...3A **32**
Breamore Hants ...2C **29**
Brean Som ...1B **14**
Bremhill Wilts ...2A **8**
Brent Knoll Som ...1C **15**
Briantspuddle Dors ...1D **37**
Bridge Som ...3C **25**
Bridgehampton Som ...1A **26**
Bridgemary Hants ...3C **31**
Bridgeyate S Glo ...2B **6**
Bridgwater Som ...3C **15**
Bridport Dors ...1D **35**
Brighstone IOW ...2B **40**
Brighton Hill Hants ...2D **21**
Brightwalton W Ber ...2B **10**
Brightwalton Green W Ber ...2B **10**
Brightwell-cum-Sotwell Oxon ...1C **11**
Brigmerston Wilts ...2C **19**
Brimpton W Ber ...3C **11**
Brinkworth Wilts ...1B **8**
Brinscombe Som ...1D **15**
Brislington Bris ...3A **6**
Bristol Bris ...**44** (2A **6**)
Bristol Airport N Som ...3A **6**

Britford Wilts ...1C **29**
Britwell Salome Oxon ...1D **11**
Brixton Deverill Wilts ...3D **17**
Broad Blunsdon Swin ...1C **9**
Broadbridge W Sus ...3B **32**
Broadbridge Heath W Sus ...3D **23**
Broad Chalke Wilts ...1B **28**
Broadford Bridge W Sus ...1D **33**
Broadhembury Devn ...3A **24**
Broad Hinton Wilts ...2C **9**
Broad Laying Hants ...3B **10**
Broadmayne Dors ...2C **37**
Broadmere Hants ...2D **21**
Broad Oak Dors ...2C **27**
Broad Oak Devn ...1A **34**
Broadoak Dors ...1D **35**
Broadoak Hants ...2C **31**
Broadshard Som ...2D **25**
Broadstone Pool ...1B **38**
Broad Town Wilts ...2B **8**
Broadway Som ...2C **25**
Broadwey Dors ...2B **36**
Broadwindsor Dors ...3D **25**
Brockbridge Hants ...2D **31**
Brockenhurst Hants ...3D **29**
Brockhurst Hants ...3C **31**
Brockley N Som ...3D **5**
Brokenborough Wilts ...1A **8**
Bromham Wilts ...3A **8**
Brompton Ralph Som ...3A **14**
Brook Hants ...2D **29**
...(nr Cadnam)
Brook Hants ...1A **30**
...(nr Romsey)
Brook Surr ...2D **23**
...(nr Guildford)
Brook Surr ...3C **23**
...(nr Haslemere)
Brook IOW ...2A **40**
Brooks Green W Sus ...1D **33**
Brookwood Surr ...1C **23**
Broomer's Corner W Sus ...1D **33**
Broomfield Som ...3B **14**
Broomhall Wind ...3C **13**
Broom Hill Dors ...3B **28**
Broughton Hants ...3A **20**
Broughton Gifford Wilts ...3D **7**
Brown Candover Hants ...3C **21**
Brunton Wilts ...1D **19**
Bruton Som ...3B **16**
Bryanston Dors ...3D **27**
Brympton D'Evercy Som ...2A **26**
Buckerell Devn ...3A **24**
Buckhorn Weston Dors ...1C **27**
Buckland Dinham Som ...1C **17**
Buckland Newton Dors ...3B **26**
Buckland Ripers Dors ...2B **36**
Buckland St Mary Som ...2B **24**
Bucklebury W Ber ...2C **11**
Buckler's Hard Hants ...1B **40**
Bucks Green W Sus ...3D **23**
Bucks Horn Oak Hants ...2B **22**
Budleigh Salterton Devn ...2A **34**
Bulford Wilts ...2C **19**
Bulford Camp Wilts ...2C **19**
Bulkington Wilts ...1A **18**
Bull Hill Hants ...1A **40**
Burbage Wilts ...3D **9**
Burchett's Green Wind ...1B **12**
Burcombe Wilts ...3B **18**
Burcott Som ...2A **16**
Burghclere Hants ...3B **10**
Burghfield W Ber ...3D **11**
Burghfield Common W Ber ...3D **11**
Burghfield Hill W Ber ...3D **11**
Buriton Hants ...1A **32**
Burleigh Wind ...2B **12**
Burlescombe Devn ...2A **24**
Burleston Dors ...1C **37**
Burley Hants ...3D **29**
Burley Street Hants ...3D **29**
Burnett Bath ...3B **6**
Burnham Buck ...1C **13**
Burnham-on-Sea Som ...2C **15**
Burntcommon Surr ...1D **23**
Burnt Hill W Ber ...2C **11**
Burpham Surr ...1D **23**
Burpham W Sus ...3D **33**
Burridge Hants ...2C **31**
Burridge Som ...3C **25**
Burrington N Som ...1D **15**
Burrow Devn ...2A **34**
Burrowbridge Som ...1C **25**
Burrowhill Surr ...3C **13**
Burslodge Hants ...3B **30**
Burstock Dors ...3D **25**
Burtle Som ...2D **15**

Burton Dors ...1C **39**
...(nr Christchurch)
Burton Dors ...1B **36**
...(nr Dorchester)
Burton Wilts ...2D **7**
...(nr Chippenham)
Burton Wilts ...3D **17**
...(nr Warminster)
Burton Som ...2A **14**
Burton Bradstock Dors ...2D **35**
Bury W Sus ...2D **33**
Busbridge Surr ...2C **23**
Bushey Dors ...2A **38**
Bushton Wilts ...2B **8**
Bussex Som ...3C **15**
Butcombe N Som ...3A **6**
Butleigh Som ...3A **16**
Butleigh Wootton Som ...3A **16**
Butlocks Heath Hants ...3B **30**
Buttermere Wilts ...3A **10**
Buttsash Hants ...3B **30**
Byfleet Surr ...3D **13**
Byworth W Sus ...1C **33**

C

Cadley Wilts ...1D **19**
...(nr Ludgershall)
Cadley Wilts ...3D **9**
...(nr Marlborough)
Cadmore End Buck ...1A **12**
Cadnam Hants ...2D **29**
Caerau Card ...2A **4**
Caerdydd Card ...**44** (2A **4**)
Caerffili Cphy ...1A **4**
Caerleon Newp ...1C **5**
Caerllion Newp ...1C **5**
Caerphilly Cphy ...1A **4**
Caerwent Mon ...1D **5**
Calbourne IOW ...2B **40**
Calcot Row W Ber ...2D **11**
Caldicot Mon ...1D **5**
Callow Hill Wilts ...1B **8**
Calmore Hants ...2A **30**
Calne Wilts ...2A **8**
Calshot Hants ...3B **30**
Calstone Wellington Wilts ...3B **8**
Camberley Surr ...3B **12**
Cameley Bath ...1B **16**
Camelsdale W Sus ...3B **22**
Camerton Bath ...1B **16**
Canada Hants ...2D **29**
Cane End Oxon ...2D **11**
Canford Cliffs Pool ...2B **38**
Canford Heath Pool ...1B **38**
Canford Magna Pool ...1B **38**
Cann Dors ...1D **27**
Cann Common Dors ...1D **27**
Cannington Som ...3B **14**
Canton Card ...2A **4**
Capel Llanilltern Card ...2A **4**
Capton Som ...3A **14**
Cardiff Card ...**44** (2A **4**)
Cardiff Airport V Glam ...3A **4**
Carisbrooke IOW ...2B **40**
Carlingcott Bath ...1B **16**
Carrow Hill Mon ...1D **5**
Cartbridge Surr ...1D **23**
Carter's Clay Hants ...1A **30**
Cas-gwent Mon ...1A **6**
Cashmoor Dors ...2A **28**
Casnewydd Newp ...1C **5**
Castell-y-bwch Torf ...1B **4**
Castle Som ...2A **16**
Castle Cary Som ...3B **16**
Castle Combe Wilts ...2D **7**
Castle Green Surr ...3C **13**
Castleton Newp ...1B **4**
Castletown Dors ...3B **36**
Catcott Som ...3C **15**
Catherington Hants ...2D **31**
Catherston Leweston Dors ...1C **35**
Catisfield Hants ...3C **31**
Catmore W Ber ...1B **10**
Cat's Ash Newp ...1C **5**
Catsgore Som ...1A **26**
Catteshall Surr ...2C **23**
Cattistock Dors ...1A **36**
Caversham Read ...2A **12**
Caversham Heights Read ...2A **12**
Cerne Abbas Dors ...3B **26**
Chaddleworth W Ber ...2B **10**
Chaffcombe Som ...2C **25**
Chalbury Dors ...3B **28**
Chalbury Common Dors ...3B **28**
Chaldon Herring Dors ...2C **37**
Chale IOW ...3B **40**

Chale Green *IOW* 3B **40**
Chalfont Common *Buck*....................1D **13**
Chalfont St Giles *Buck*....................1C **13**
Chalfont St Peter *Buck*.................1D **13**
Chalton *Hants*................................2A **32**
Chandler's Ford *Hants*...................1B **30**
Chantry *Som*..................................2C **17**
Chapel Allerton *Som*......................1D **15**
Chapel Row *W Ber*.........................3C **11**
Chapmanslade *Wilts*......................2D **17**
Chard *Som*..................................3C **25**
Chard Junction *Dors*......................3C **25**
Chardstock *Devn*............................3C **25**
Charfield *S Glo*...............................1C **7**
Charlcombe *Bath*...........................3C **7**
Charlcutt *Wilts*..............................2A **8**
Charleshill *Surr*..............................2B **22**
Charlestown *Dors*..........................3B **36**
Charlton *Hants*..............................2A **20**
Charlton *Oxon*...............................1B **10**
Charlton *Som*................................1B **16**
...................................(nr Radstock)
Charlton *Som*................................2B **16**
...............................(nr Shepton Mallet)
Charlton *Som*................................1B **24**
.... (nr Taunton)
Charlton *W Sus*.............................2B **32**
Charlton *Wilts*...............................1A **8**
.................................(nr Malmesbury)
Charlton *Wilts*...............................1C **19**
.....................................(nr Pewsey)
Charlton *Wilts*...............................1A **28**
..................................(nr Shaftesbury)
Charlton Adam *Som*.......................1A **26**
Charlton All Saints *Wilts*................1C **29**
Charlton Down *Dors*.......................1B **36**
Charlton Horethorne *Som*...............1B **26**
Charlton Mackrell *Som*...................1A **26**
Charlton Marshall *Dors*..................3A **28**
Charlton Musgrove *Som*.................1C **27**
Charlton on the Hill *Dors*................3D **27**
Charlwood *Hants*...........................3D **21**
Charlynch *Som*...............................3B **14**
Charminster *Dors*..........................1B **36**
Charmouth *Dors*............................1C **35**
Charter Alley *Hants*.......................1C **21**
Charterhouse *Som*.........................1D **15**
Charvil *Wok*...................................2A **12**
Chawton *Hants*.............................3A **22**
Cheapside *Wind*............................3C **13**
Checkendon *Oxon*.........................1D **11**
Cheddar *Som*.................................1D **15**
Cheddon Fitzpaine *Som*.................1B **24**
Chedglow *Wilts*.............................1A **8**
Chedington *Dors*...........................3D **25**
Chedzoy *Som*................................3C **15**
Chelston *Som*................................1A **24**
Chelvey *N Som*..............................3D **5**
Chelwood *Bath*.............................3B **6**
Chelworth Lower Green *Wilts*.........1B **8**
Chelworth Upper Green *Wilts*.........1B **8**
Chelynch *Som*................................2B **16**
Chepstow *Mon*............................1A **6**
Cherhill *Wilts*................................2B **8**
Cheriton *Hants*..............................1C **31**
Chertsey *Surr*.............................3D **13**
Cheselbourne *Dors*........................1C **37**
Chesterblade *Som*.........................2B **16**
Chetnole *Dors*...............................3B **26**
Chettle *Dors*.................................2A **28**
Chew Magna *Bath*.........................3A **6**
Chew Stoke *Bath*..........................3A **6**
Chewton Keynsham *Bath*...............3B **6**
Chewton Mendip *Som*....................1A **16**
Chichester *W Sus*.......................3B **32**
Chickerell *Dors*.............................2B **36**
Chicklade *Wilts*.............................3A **18**
Chidden *Hants*..............................2D **31**
Chiddingfold *Surr*..........................3C **23**
Chideock *Dors*...............................1D **35**
Chidgley *Som*................................3A **14**
Chidham *W Sus*.............................3A **32**
Chieveley *W Ber*............................2B **10**
Chilbolton *Hants*...........................2A **20**
Chilcomb *Hants*............................1C **31**
Chilcombe *Dors*............................1A **36**
Chilcompton *Som*..........................1B **16**
Child Okeford *Dors*........................2D **27**
Childrey *Oxon*...............................1A **10**
Chilfrome *Dors*..............................1A **36**
Chilgrove *W Sus*............................2B **32**
Chilhampton *Wilts*.........................3B **18**
Chilland *Hants*..............................3C **21**
Chillerton *IOW*...............................2B **40**
Chillington *Som*............................2C **25**
Chilmark *Wilts*...............................3A **18**
Chilthorne Domer *Som*...................2A **26**

Chilton *Oxon*.................................1B **10**
Chilton Candover *Hants*.................2C **21**
Chilton Cantelo *Som*......................1A **26**
Chilton Foliat *Wilts*........................2A **10**
Chilton Polden *Som*.......................3C **15**
Chilton Trinity *Som*........................3B **14**
Chilworth *Hants*............................2B **30**
Chilworth *Surr*...............................2D **23**
Chineham *Hants*............................1D **21**
Chipley *Som*..................................1A **24**
Chippenham *Wilts*......................2A **8**
Chipping Sodbury *S Glo*.............1C **7**
Chipstable *Som*.............................1A **24**
Chirton *Wilts*.................................1B **18**
Chisbridge Cross *Buck*...................1B **12**
Chisbury *Wilts*...............................3D **9**
Chiselborough *Som*........................2D **25**
Chiseldon *Swin*.............................2C **9**
Chiswell *Dors*................................3B **36**
Chithurst *W Sus*............................1B **32**
Chitterne *Wilts*.............................2A **18**
Chittoe *Wilts*.................................3A **8**
Chobham *Surr*...............................3C **13**
Cholderton *Wilts*...........................2D **19**
Cholsey *Oxon*................................1C **11**
Christchurch *Dors*......................1C **39**
Christian Malford *Wilts*...................2A **8**
Christmas Common *Oxon*..............1A **12**
Christon *N Som*.............................1C **15**
Church Crookham *Hants*................1B **22**
Church End *Hants*.........................1D **21**
Church End *Wilts*...........................2B **8**
Church Green *Devn*........................1A **34**
Churchill *Devn*...............................3C **25**
Churchill *N Som*.............................1D **15**
Churchinford *Som*..........................2B **24**
Church Knowle *Dors*......................2A **38**
Church Norton *W Sus*.....................1B **42**
Churchstanton *Som*.......................2A **24**
Church Village *Rhon*......................1A **4**
Churt *Surr*.....................................3B **22**
Chute Standen *Wilts*......................1A **20**
Cilfrynydd *Rhon*............................1A **4**
Cippenham *Slo*.............................1C **13**
Clandown *Bath*.............................1B **16**
Clanfield *Hants*.............................2D **31**
Clanville *Hants*..............................2A **20**
Clanville *Som*................................3B **16**
Clapgate *Dors*...............................3B **28**
Clapham *W Sus*.............................3D **33**
Clapton *Som*.................................3D **25**
.... (nr Crewkerne)
Clapton *Som*.................................1B **16**
.... (nr Radstock)
Clapton in Gordano *N Som*.............2D **5**
Clatterford *IOW*..............................2B **40**
Clatworthy *Som*.............................3A **14**
Claverham *N Som*..........................3D **5**
Claverton *Bath*.............................3C **7**
Clawdd-côch *V Glam*.......................2A **4**
Claygate *Surr*................................3D **13**
Clayhall *Hants*...............................1D **41**
Clayhidon *Devn*.............................2A **24**
Clay Hill *Bris*.................................2B **6**
Clayhill *Hants*................................3A **30**
Cleeve *N Som*...............................3D **5**
Cleeve *Oxon*..................................1D **11**
Clench Common *Wilts*....................3C **9**
Clevancy *Wilts*...............................2B **8**
Clevedon *N Som*.........................2D **5**
Cleverton *Wilts*..............................1A **8**
Clewer *Som*...................................1D **15**
Cliddesden *Hants*..........................2D **21**
Clifton *Bris*....................................2A **6**
Climping *W Sus*.............................3C **33**
Clink *Som*......................................2C **17**
Cloford *Som*..................................2C **17**
Closworth *Som*..............................2A **26**
Clutton *Bath*.................................1B **16**
Clyffe Pypard *Wilts*........................2B **8**
Coalpit Heath *S Glo*.......................1B **6**
Coat *Som*......................................1D **25**
Coate *Swin*....................................1C **9**
Coate *Wilts*...................................3B **8**
Coates *W Sus*................................2C **33**
Cobham *Surr*.............................1D **23**
Cocking *W Sus*..............................2B **32**
Cocking Causeway *W Sus*..............2B **32**
Cocklake *Som*...............................2D **15**
Cockpole Green *Wok*.....................1A **12**
Codford *Wilts*................................3A **18**
Codmore Hill *W Sus*......................1D **33**
Codrington *S Glo*..........................2C **7**
Coedkernew *Newp*........................1B **4**
Cogan *V Glam*...............................2A **4**
Colaton Raleigh *Devn*....................2A **34**
Cold Ash *W Ber*.............................3C **11**

Cold Ashton *S Glo*.........................2C **7**
Colden Common *Hants*..................1B **30**
Cold Harbour *Dors*........................1A **38**
Coldharbour *Surr*..........................2D **23**
Coldwaltham *W Sus*......................2D **33**
Cole *Som*......................................3B **16**
Coleford *Som*................................2B **16**
Cole Henley *Hants*........................1B **20**
Colehill *Dors*.................................3B **28**
Colemore *Hants*............................3A **22**
Colerne *Wilts*................................2D **7**
Coleshill *Oxon*..............................1D **9**
Colestocks *Devn*...........................3A **24**
Coley *Bath*....................................1A **16**
Collingbourne Ducis *Wilts*..............1D **19**
Collingbourne Kingston *Wilts*.........1A **19**
Colliton *Devn*.................................3A **24**
Colnbrook *Slo*................................2D **13**
Colworth *W Sus*............................3C **33**
Colyford *Devn*...............................1B **34**
Colyton *Devn*.................................1B **34**
Combe *W Ber*................................3A **10**
Combe Almer *Dors*........................1A **38**
Combe Down *Bath*.........................3C **7**
Combe Florey *Som*........................3A **14**
Combe Hay *Bath*............................3C **7**
Combe Raleigh *Devn*......................3A **24**
Combe St Nicholas *Som*.................2C **25**
Combpyne *Devn*............................1B **34**
Combwich *Som*..............................2B **14**
Common, The *Wilts*........................3D **19**
....................................(nr Salisbury)
Common, The *Wilts*........................1B **8**
.... (nr Swindon)
Compton *Hants*.............................1B **30**
Compton *Surr*................................2C **23**
Compton *W Ber*.............................2C **11**
Compton *W Sus*.............................2A **32**
Compton *Wilts*...............................1C **19**
Compton Abbas *Dors*....................2D **27**
Compton Bassett *Wilts*..................2B **8**
Compton Beauchamp *Oxon*...........1D **9**
Compton Bishop *Som*....................1C **15**
Compton Chamberlayne *Wilts*........1B **28**
Compton Dando *Bath*.....................3B **6**
Compton Dundon *Som*...................3D **15**
Compton Greenfield *S Glo*.............1A **6**
Compton Martin *Bath*.....................1A **16**
Compton Pauncefoot *Som*.............1B **26**
Compton Valence *Dors*..................1A **36**
Coneyhurst *W Sus*.........................1D **33**
Conford *Hants*...............................3B **22**
Congresbury *N Som*.......................3D **5**
Conham *S Glo*...............................2B **6**
Conock *Wilts*.................................1B **18**
Cookham *Wind*..............................1B **12**
Cookham Dean *Wind*.....................1B **12**
Cookham Rise *Wind*.......................1B **12**
Cookley Green *Oxon*.....................1D **11**
Coolham *W Sus*.............................1D **33**
Coombe *Devn*...............................1A **34**
Coombe *Glos*................................1C **7**
Coombe *Hants*..............................1D **31**
Coombe *Wilts*................................1C **19**
Coombe Bissett *Wilts*....................1C **29**
Coombe Keynes *Dors*....................2D **37**
Cootham *W Sus*.............................2D **33**
Copythorne *Hants*.........................2A **30**
Corfe *Som*.....................................2B **24**
Corfe Castle *Dors*.........................2A **38**
Corfe Mullen *Dors*........................1A **38**
Corhampton *Hants*........................1D **31**
Corscombe *Dors*...........................3A **26**
Corsham *Wilts*..........................2D **7**
Corsley *Wilts*................................2D **17**
Corsley Heath *Wilts*......................2D **17**
Corston *Bath*.................................3B **6**
Corston *Wilts*.................................1A **8**
Corton *Wilts*..................................1A **18**
Corton Denham *Som*......................1B **26**
Coryates *Dors*...............................2B **36**
Coscote *Oxon*................................1C **11**
Cosham *Port*.................................3D **31**
Cosmeston *V Glam*........................3A **4**
Cossington *Som*............................2C **15**
Cotford St Luke *Som*......................1A **24**
Cothelstone *Som*...........................3A **14**
Cotleigh *Devn*...............................3B **24**
Coulston *Wilts*...............................1A **18**
Coultings *Som*...............................2B **14**
Countess *Wilts*..............................2C **19**
Courtway *Som*...............................3B **14**
Cove *Hants*...................................1B **22**
Covingham *Swin*...........................1C **9**
Cowes *IOW*................................1B **40**
Cowley *G Lon*................................1D **13**
Cowplain *Hants*.............................2D **31**

Cowslip Green *N Som*....................3D **5**
Cox Green *Surr*.............................3D **23**
Coxley *Som*...................................2A **16**
Crab Orchard *Dors*........................3B **28**
Craddock *Devn*.............................2A **24**
Cranborne *Dors*............................2B **28**
Cranbourne *Brac*...........................2C **13**
Cranford *G Lon*.............................2D **13**
Cranleigh *Surr*..........................3D **23**
Cranmore *IOW*..............................1B **40**
Crawley *Devn*................................3B **24**
Crawley *Hants*..............................3B **20**
Cray's Pond *Oxon*.........................1D **11**
Crazies Hill *Wok*...........................1A **12**
Creech *Dors*..................................2A **38**
Creech Heathfield *Som*..................1B **24**
Creech St Michael *Som*.................1B **24**
Creekmoor *Pool*............................1A **38**
Creigiau *Card*................................1A **4**
Crendell *Dors*................................2B **28**
Crewkerne *Som*............................3D **25**
Cribbs Causeway *S Glo*.................1A **6**
Crick *Mon*.....................................1D **5**
Cricket Hill *Hants*..........................3B **12**
Cricket Malherbie *Som*...................2C **25**
Cricket St Thomas *Som*.................3C **25**
Crickham *Som*...............................2D **15**
Cricklade *Wilts*..............................1C **9**
Crimchard *Som*.............................3C **25**
Cripplestyle *Dors*..........................2B **28**
Crocker End *Oxon*.........................1A **12**
Crockerhill *Hants*...........................3C **31**
Crockerton *Wilts*...........................2D **17**
Croes-y-mwyalch *Torf*....................1C **5**
Croford *Som*..................................1A **24**
Crofton *Wilts*.................................3D **9**
Cromhall *S Glo*..............................1B **6**
Crondall *Hants*..............................2A **22**
Crooked Soley *Wilts*......................2A **10**
Crookham *W Ber*...........................3C **11**
Crookham Village *Hants*................1A **22**
Croscombe *Som*............................2A **16**
Cross *Som*.....................................1D **15**
Crossbush *W Sus*..........................3D **33**
Cross Inn *Rhon*.............................1A **4**
Crosskeys *Cphy*............................1B **4**
Crossways *Dors*............................2C **37**
Croucheston *Wilts*.........................1B **28**
Crouch Hill *Dors*...........................2C **27**
Crow *Hants*...................................3C **29**
Crowcombe *Som*...........................3A **14**
Crowdhill *Hants*.............................2B **30**
Crowmarsh Gifford *Oxon*...............1D **11**
Crowthorne *Brac*.......................3B **12**
Crudwell *Wilts*...............................1A **8**
Crux Easton *Hants*........................1B **20**
Cruxton *Dors*.................................1B **36**
Cucklington *Som*...........................1C **27**
Cudworth *Som*...............................2C **25**
Culm Davy *Devn*............................2A **24**
Culmstock *Devn*.............................2A **24**
Cupernham *Hants*.........................1A **30**
Curbridge *Hants*............................2C **31**
Curdridge *Hants*............................2C **31**
Curland *Som*..................................2B **24**
Curland Common *Som*...................2B **24**
Curridge *W Ber*.............................2B **10**
Curry Mallet *Som*..........................1C **25**
Curry Rivel *Som*............................1C **25**
Cuttiford's Door *Som*.....................2C **25**
Cwmcarn *Cphy*..............................1B **4**
Cwmfelinfach *Cphy*.......................1A **4**
Cyncoed *Card*...............................1A **4**

D

Daggons *Dors*...............................2C **29**
Dalwood *Devn*..............................3B **24**
Damerham *Hants*..........................2C **29**
Daneshill *Hants*............................1D **21**
Datchet *Wind*................................2C **13**
Dauntsey *Wilts*.............................1A **8**
Dauntsey Green *Wilts*....................1A **8**
Dauntsey Lock *Wilts*......................1A **8**
Dean *Hants*...................................2C **31**
.............................(nr Bishop's Waltham)
Dean *Hants*...................................3B **20**
.....................................(nr Winchester)
Dean *Dors*.....................................2A **28**
Dean *Som*.....................................2B **16**
Deane *Hants*.................................1C **21**
Deanland *Dors*..............................2A **28**
Deanlane End *W Sus*......................2A **32**
Deepcut *Surr*.................................1C **23**
Denchworth *Oxon*.........................1A **10**
Denham *Buck*................................1D **13**
Denham Green *Buck*......................1D **13**

Denmead *Hants*...................2D **31**
Deptford *Wilts*.....................3B **18**
Derry Hill *Wilts*...................2A **8**
Devizes *Wilts*.....................3B **8**
Dewlish *Dors*........................1C **37**
Dial Green *W Sus*..............1C **33**
Dial Post *W Sus*.................2D **33**
Dibberford *Dors*..................3D **25**
Dibden *Hants*......................3B **30**
Dibden Purlieu *Hants*.........3B **30**
Didcot *Oxon*......................1C **11**
Didling *W Sus*.....................2B **32**
Didmarton *Glos*...................1D **7**
Dilton Marsh *Wilts*..............2D **17**
Dimmer *Som*........................3B **16**
Dinas Powys *V Glam*..........2A **4**
Dinder *Som*..........................2A **16**
Dinnington *Som*...................2D **25**
Dinton *Wilts*.........................3B **18**
Dipley *Hants*........................1A **22**
Dippenhall *Surr*...................2B **22**
Ditchampton *Wilts*...............3B **18**
Ditcheat *Som*.......................3B **16**
Ditteridge *Wilts*...................3D **7**
Dodington *S Glo*..................1C **7**
Dodington *Som*....................2A **14**
Dogmersfield *Hants*............1A **22**
Donhead St Andrew *Wilts*...1A **28**
Donhead St Mary *Wilts*......1A **28**
Doniford *Som*.......................2A **14**
Donkey Town *Surr*...............3C **13**
Donnington *W Ber*...............3B **10**
Donnington *W Sus*...............3B **32**
Donyatt *Som*........................2C **25**
Dorchester *Dors*..............1B **36**
Dorney *Buck*........................2C **13**
Dottery *Dors*........................1D **35**
Doughton *Glos*....................1D **7**
Doulting *Som*.......................2B **16**
Dowlands *Devn*...................1B **34**
Dowlesgreen *Wok*..............3B **12**
Dowlish Wake *Som*.............2C **25**
Downend *IOW*.....................2C **41**
Downend *S Glo*...................2B **6**
Downend *W Ber*..................2B **10**
Downhead *Som*....................2B **16**
....(nr Frome)
Downhead *Som*....................1A **26**
....(nr Yeovil)
Downside *Som*.....................1B **16**
....(nr Chilcompton)
Downside *Som*.....................2B **16**
...................................(nr Shepton Mallet)
Downside *Surr*.....................1D **23**
Downton *Hants*....................1D **39**
Downton *Wilts*.....................1C **29**
Doynton *S Glo*.....................2C **7**
Draethen *Cphy*....................1B **4**
Dragon's Green *W Sus*.......1D **33**
Draycot Foliat *Swin*.............2C **9**
Draycott *Som*.......................1D **15**
....(nr Cheddar)
Draycott *Som*.......................1A **26**
....(nr Yeovil)
Drayton Port..........................3D **31**
Drayton *Som*........................1D **25**
Drimpton *Dors*.....................3D **25**
Droop *Dors*..........................3C **27**
Drope *V Glam*......................2A **4**
Droxford *Hants*....................2D **31**
Duck Street *Hants*...............2A **20**
Dulcote *Som*........................2A **16**
Dulford *Devn*........................3A **24**
Dummer *Hants*.....................2C **21**
Dumpford *W Sus*.................1B **32**
Dunball *Som*........................2C **15**
Dunbridge *Hants*.................1A **30**
Duncton *W Sus*...................2C **33**
Dundon *Som*........................3D **15**
Dundridge *Hants*.................2C **31**
Dundry *N Som*......................3A **6**
Dunge *Wilts*.........................1D **17**
Dunkerton *Bath*...................1C **17**
Dunkeswell *Devn*................3A **24**
Dunkirk *S Glo*......................1C **7**
Dunkirk *Wilts*.......................3A **8**
Dunley *Hants*.......................1B **20**
Dunsden Green *Oxon*..........2A **12**
Dunsfold *Surr*......................3D **23**
Duntish *Dors*........................3B **26**
Durleigh *Som*.......................3B **14**
Durley *Hants*........................2C **31**
Durley *Wilts*.........................3D **9**
Durley Street *Hants*............2C **31**
Durns Town *Hants*...............1D **39**
Durrants *Hants*....................2A **32**
Durrington *W Sus*................3D **33**

Durrington *Wilts*...................2C **19**
Durston *Som*.......................1B **24**
Durweston *Dors*...................3D **27**
Dyffryn *V Glam*....................2A **4**
Dyrham *S Glo*......................2C **7**

E

Earley *Wok*...........................2A **12**
Earnley *W Sus*.....................1B **42**
Eartham *W Sus*....................3C **33**
Earthcott Green *S Glo*.........1B **6**
Easebourne *W Sus*..............1B **32**
Eashing *Surr*........................2C **23**
East Anton *Hants*.................2A **20**
East Ashling *W Sus*.............3B **32**
East Aston *Hants*.................2B **20**
East Beach *W Sus*...............1B **42**
East Bedfont *G Lon*.............2D **13**
East Bloxworth *Dors*...........1D **37**
East Boldre *Hants*...............3A **30**
East Brent *Som*....................1C **15**
East Budleigh *Devn*.............2A **34**
East Burnham *Buck*.............1C **13**
East Burton *Dors*.................2D **37**
Eastbury *Herts*....................1D **13**
Eastbury *W Ber*...................2A **10**
East Chaldon *Dors*..............2C **37**
East Challow *Oxon*..............1A **10**
East Chelborough *Dors*.......3A **26**
East Chinnock *Som*.............2D **25**
East Chisenbury *Wilts*.........1C **19**
East Clandon *Surr*...............1D **23**
East Clevedon *N Som*.........2D **5**
East Coker *Som*...................2A **26**
East Combe *Som*.................3A **14**
East Compton *Som*..............2B **16**
Eastcote *G Lon*....................1D **13**
Eastcott *Wilts*......................1B **18**
Eastcourt *Wilts*....................3D **9**
....(nr Pewsey)
Eastcourt *Wilts*....................1A **8**
....(nr Tetbury)
East Cowes *IOW*.................1C **41**
East Cranmore *Som*............2B **16**
East Creech *Dors*................2A **38**
East Dean *Hants*.................1D **29**
East Dean *W Sus*.................2C **33**
East Dundry *N Som*.............3A **6**
East End *Dors*......................1A **38**
East End *Hants*....................1A **40**
.....................................(nr Lymington)
East End *Hants*....................3B **10**
....(nr Newbury)
East End *N Som*...................2D **5**
East End *Som*......................1A **16**
Easter Compton *S Glo*........1A **6**
Eastergate *W Sus*...............3C **33**
Easterton *Wilts*....................1B **18**
Eastertown *Som*..................1C **15**
East Everleigh *Wilts*............1D **19**
East Garston *W Ber*.............2A **10**
East Ginge *Oxon*.................1B **10**
East Grafton *Wilts*...............3D **9**
East Grimstead *Wilts*...........1D **29**
East Hagbourne *Oxon*.........1C **11**
Easthampstead *Brac*...........3B **12**
East Hanney *Oxon*...............1B **10**
East Harptree *Bath*..............1A **16**
East Harting *W Sus*.............2B **32**
East Hatch *Wilts*..................1A **28**
Eastheath *Wok*....................3B **12**
East Hendred *Oxon*.............1B **10**
East Holme *Dors*.................2D **37**
East Horrington *Som*...........2A **16**
East Horsley *Surr*................1D **23**
East Howe *Bour*...................1B **38**
East Huntspill *Som*..............2C **15**
East Ilsley *W Ber*.................1B **10**
East Kennett *Wilts*...............3C **9**
East Knighton *Dors*.............2D **37**
East Knoyle *Wilts*................3D **17**
East Lambrook *Som*............2D **25**
East Lavant *W Sus*..............3B **32**
East Lavington *W Sus*.........2C **33**
Eastleigh *Hants*...............2B **30**
East Liss *Hants*....................1A **32**
East Lockinge *Oxon*............1B **10**
East Lulworth *Dors*.............2D **37**
East Lydford *Som*................3A **16**
East Lyng *Som*....................1C **25**
East Marden *W Sus*.............2B **32**
East Meon *Hants*.................1D **31**
East Molesey *Surr*...............3D **13**
East Morden *Dors*................1A **38**
Eastney *Port*........................1D **41**
East Nynehead *Som*............1A **24**

East Oakley *Hants*...............1C **21**
Easton *Dors*.........................3B **36**
Easton *Hants*.......................3C **21**
Easton *Som*.........................2A **16**
Easton *Wilts*.........................2D **7**
Easton Grey *Wilts*...............1D **7**
Easton-in-Gordano *N Som*...2A **6**
Easton Royal *Wilts*..............3D **9**
East Orchard *Dors*..............2D **27**
East Pennard *Som*...............3A **16**
East Preston *W Sus*............3D **33**
East Shefford *W Ber*...........2A **10**
East Stoke *Dors*..................2D **37**
East Stoke *Som*...................2D **25**
East Stour *Dors*...................1D **27**
East Stratton *Hants*.............2C **21**
East Tisted *Hants*................3A **22**
East Tytherley *Hants*...........1D **29**
East Tytherton *Wilts*............2A **8**
East Wellow *Hants*..............1A **30**
East Winterslow *Wilts*.........3D **19**
East Wittering *W Sus*..........1A **42**
East Woodhay *Hants*...........3B **10**
East Woodlands *Som*..........2C **17**
East Worldham *Hants*.........3A **22**
Ebbesbourne Wake *Wilts*....1A **28**
Ebblake *Dors*......................3C **29**
Ebernoe *W Sus*...................1C **33**
Ecchinswell *Hants*...............1C **21**
Eddington *W Ber*.................3A **10**
Edgarley *Som*......................3A **16**
Edgington *Som*....................3C **15**
Edgington *Wilts*...................1A **18**
Edingworth *Som*..................1C **15**
Edithmead *Som*...................2C **15**
Edmondsham *Dors*..............2B **28**
Efail Isaf *Rhon*.....................1A **4**
Effingham *Surr*....................1D **23**
Effingham Common *Surr*.....1D **23**
Egbury *Hants*.......................1B **20**
Egham *Surr*.....................2D **13**
Egham Hythe *Surr*...............2D **13**
Egypt *Buck*..........................1C **13**
Egypt *Hants*.........................2B **20**
Elberton *S Glo*.....................1B **6**
Elbridge *W Sus*....................3C **33**
Elcombe *Swin*......................1C **9**
Elcot *W Ber*..........................3A **10**
Eling *Hants*...........................2A **30**
Eling *W Ber*..........................2C **11**
Ellen's Green *Surr*...............3D **23**
Ellingham *Hants*..................3C **29**
Ellisfield *Hants*....................2D **21**
Elmfield *IOW*........................1D **41**
Elm Hill *Dors*........................1D **27**
Elstead *Surr*.........................2C **23**
Elsted *W Sus*.......................2B **32**
Elsted Marsh *W Sus*............1B **32**
Elston *Wilts*..........................2B **18**
Elvetham Heath *Hants*.........1A **22**
Elworth *Dors*........................2A **36**
Elworthy *Som*.......................3A **14**
Ely *Card*...............................2A **4**
Emborough *Som*..................1B **16**
Emery Down *Hants*..............3D **29**
Emmbrook *Wok*....................3A **12**
Emmer Green *Read*.............2A **12**
Empshott *Hants*...................3A **22**
Emsworth *Hants*..............3A **32**
Enborne *W Ber*....................3B **10**
Enborne Row *W Ber*............3B **10**
Enford *Wilts*..........................1C **19**
Engine Common *S Glo*........1B **6**
Englefield *W Ber*..................2D **11**
Englefield Green *Surr*..........2C **13**
Englishcombe *Bath*.............3C **7**
Enham Alamein *Hants*.........2A **20**
Enmore *Som*........................3B **14**
Ensbury *Bour*.......................1B **38**
Erlestoke *Wilts*.....................1A **18**
Esher *Surr*.......................3D **13**
Etchilhampton *Wilts*.............3B **8**
Eton *Wind*.............................2C **13**
Eton Wick *Wind*...................2C **13**
Even Swindon *Swin*.............1C **9**
Evercreech *Som*..................3B **16**
Evergreen *Wilts*...................1D **19**
Evershot *Dors*......................3A **26**
Eversley *Hants*.....................3A **12**
Eversley Cen. *Hants*............3A **12**
Eversley Cross *Hants*..........3A **12**
Everton *Hants*......................1D **39**
Ewelme *Oxon*.......................1D **11**
Ewhurst *Surr*........................2D **23**
Ewhurst Green *Surr*............3D **23**
Ewshot *Hants*.......................1B **22**

Exbury *Hants*.......................3B **30**
Exlade Street *Oxon*.............1D **11**
Exton *Hants*.........................1D **31**

F

Faccombe *Hants*..................1A **20**
Failand *N Som*......................2A **6**
Fairlands *Surr*......................1C **23**
Fairmile *Devn*.......................1A **34**
Fairmile *Surr*........................3D **13**
Fair Oak *Hants*.....................2B **30**
....(nr Eastleigh)
Fair Oak *Hants*.....................3C **11**
....(nr Kingsclere)
Fair Oak Green *Hants*.........3D **11**
Fairwater *Card*.....................2A **4**
Falfield *S Glo*.......................1B **6**
Fareham *Hants*................3C **31**
Farleigh *N Som*....................3D **5**
Farleigh Hungerford *Som*....1D **17**
Farleigh Wallop *Hants*.........2D **21**
Farleigh Wick *Wilts*.............3D **7**
Farley *Wilts*..........................1D **29**
Farley Green *Surr*................2D **23**
Farley Hill *Wok*....................3A **12**
Farlington *Port*.....................3D **31**
Farmborough *Bath*..............3B **6**
Farnborough *Hants*.........1B **22**
Farnborough *W Ber*.............1B **10**
Farncombe *Surr*...................2C **23**
Farnham *Dors*......................2A **28**
Farnham *Surr*..................2B **22**
Farnham Common *Buck*......1C **13**
Farnham Royal *Buck*...........1C **13**
Farrington *Dors*...................2D **27**
Farrington Gurney *Bath*.......1B **16**
Farway *Devn*........................1A **34**
Faulkland *Som*.....................1C **17**
Fawley *Buck*.........................1A **12**
Fawley *Hants*..................3B **30**
Fawley *W Ber*.......................1A **10**
Felpham *W Sus*....................3C **33**
Feltham *G Lon*.................2D **13**
Felthamhill *Surr*...................2D **13**
Felton *N Som*.......................3A **6**
Feniton *Devn*........................1A **34**
Fenny Bridges *Devn*............1A **34**
Ferndown *Dors*................3B **28**
Fernham *Oxon*......................1D **9**
Fernhurst *W Sus*..................1B **32**
Ferring *W Sus*......................3D **33**
Fetcham *Surr*.......................1D **23**
Ffont-y-gari *V Glam*..............3A **4**
Ffwl-y-mwn *V Glam*..............3A **4**
Fiddington *Som*....................2B **14**
Fiddleford *Dors*....................2D **27**
Fifehead Magdalen *Dors*.....1C **27**
Fifehead Neville *Dors*..........2C **27**
Fifehead St Quintin *Dors*.....2C **27**
Fifield *Wilts*...........................1C **19**
Fifield *Wind*..........................2C **13**
Fifield Bavant *Wilts*.............1B **28**
Figheldean *Wilts*..................2C **19**
Filford *Dors*..........................1D **35**
Filton *S Glo*..........................2B **6**
Finchampstead *Wok*............3A **12**
Finchdean *Hants*.................2A **32**
Findon *W Sus*.......................3D **33**
Findon Valley *W Sus*...........3D **33**
Fingest *Buck*........................1A **12**
Firsdown *Wilts*.....................3D **19**
Fishbourne *IOW*...................1C **41**
Fishbourne *W Sus*...............3B **32**
Fisher's Pond *Hants*............1B **30**
Fisherstreet *W Sus*..............3C **23**
Fisherton de la Mere *Wilts*...3A **18**
Fishpond Bottom *Dors*.........1C **35**
Fishponds *Bris*.....................2B **6**
Fittleton *Wilts*.......................2C **19**
Fittleworth *W Sus*.................2D **33**
Fitzhead *Som*.......................1A **24**
Five Bells *Som*.....................2A **14**
Fivehead *Som*......................1C **25**
Five Oaks *W Sus*.................1D **33**
Flackwell Heath *Buck*..........1B **12**
Flansham *W Sus*..................3C **33**
Flax Bourton *N Som*............3A **6**
Flaxpool *Som*.......................3A **14**
Fleet *Hants*.....................1B **22**
.....................................(nr Farnborough)
Fleet *Hants*..........................3A **32**
.....................................(nr South Hayling)
Fleet *Dors*............................2B **36**
Flexford *Surr*........................2C **23**
Fluxton *Devn*........................1A **34**
Foddington *Som*..................1A **26**

Folke *Dors*.....................................2B **26**
Fonmon *V Glam*..............................3A **4**
Fonthill Bishop *Wilts*.....................3A **18**
Fonthill Gifford *Wilts*....................3A **18**
Fontmell Magna *Dors*....................2D **27**
Fontwell *W Sus*..............................3C **33**
Font-y-gary *V Glam*.......................3A **4**
Ford *Som*......................................1A **16**
....(nr Wells)
Ford *Som*......................................1A **24**
....(nr Wiveliscombe)
Ford *W Sus*....................................3D **33**
Ford *Wilts*.....................................2D **7**
....(nr Chippenham)
Ford *Wilts*......................................3C **19**
....(nr Salisbury)
Fordingbridge *Hants*.....................2C **29**
Ford Street *Som*.............................2A **24**
Forest Green *Surr*...........................2D **23**
Forestside *W Sus*............................2A **32**
Forston *Dors*...................................1B **36**
Forton *Hants*..................................2B **20**
Forton *Som*.....................................3C **25**
Fortuneswell *Dors*..........................3B **36**
Forty Green *Buck*............................1C **13**
Fosbury *Wilts*.................................1A **20**
Four Forks *Som*...............................3B **14**
Four Marks *Hants*...........................3D **21**
Fovant *Wilts*...................................1B **28**
Fox Corner *Surr*..............................1C **23**
Foxcote *Som*...................................1C **17**
Foxham *Wilts*...................................2A **8**
Fox Lane *Hants*...............................1B **22**
Foxley *Wilts*....................................1D **7**
Frampton *Dors*................................1B **36**
Frampton Cotterell *S Glo*.................1B **6**
Fratton *Port*....................................3D **31**
Freefolk Priors *Hants*.....................2B **20**
Frenchay *S Glo*.................................2B **6**
Frensham *Surr*................................2B **22**
Freshford *Bath*.................................3C **7**
Freshwater *IOW*..............................2A **40**
Freshwater Bay *IOW*.......................2A **40**
Friar Waddon *Dors*.........................2B **36**
Friday Street *Surr*...........................2D **23**
Frieth *Buck*.....................................1A **12**
Frilsham *W Ber*...............................2C **11**
Frimley *Surr*...............................1B **22**
Frimley Green *Surr*.........................1B **22**
Fritham *Hants*................................2D **29**
Frogham *Hants*..............................2C **29**
Frogmore *Hants*........................3B **12**
Frome *Som*.................................2C **17**
Fromefield *Som*...............................2C **17**
Frome St Quintin *Dors*...................3A **26**
Froxfield *Wilts*..................................3D **9**
Froxfield Green *Hants*....................1A **32**
Fryern Hill *Hants*............................1B **30**
Fugglestone St Peter *Wilts*.............3C **19**
Fulflood *Hants*................................3B **20**
Fulford *Som*....................................1B **24**
Fullerton *Hants*..............................3A **20**
Fulmer *Buck*....................................1C **13**
Fulwood *Som*..................................2B **24**
Funtington *W Sus*...........................3B **32**
Funtley *Hants*.................................3C **31**
Furley *Devn*....................................3B **24**
Furzebrook *Dors*.............................2A **38**
Furzehill *Dors*.................................3B **28**
Furzeley Corner *Hants*...................2D **31**
Furzey Lodge *Hants*.......................3A **30**
Furzley *Hants*.................................2D **29**
Fyfield *Hants*..................................2D **19**
Fyfield *Wilts*.....................................3C **9**
Fyning *W Sus*..................................1B **32**

G

Galhampton *Som*.............................1B **26**
Gallowstree Common *Oxon*.............1D **11**
Galmington *Som*.............................1B **24**
Galton *Dors*.....................................2C **37**
Gardeners Green *Wok*.....................3B **12**
Gare Hill *Som*..................................2C **17**
Garsdon *Wilts*...................................1A **8**
Garth Place *Cphy*.............................1A **4**
Gasper *Wilts*....................................3C **17**
Gastard *Wilts*....................................3D **7**
Gatcombe *IOW*................................2B **40**
Gaunt's Common *Dors*....................3B **28**
Gaunt's Earthcott *S Glo*..................1B **6**
Gay Street *W Sus*.............................1D **33**
George Green *Buck*.........................1C **13**
Gerrards Cross *Buck*..................1C **13**
Giddeahall *Wilts*.............................2D **7**
Gillingham *Dors*..............................1D **27**
Gittisham *Devn*...............................1A **34**

Glanvilles Wootton *Dors*.................3B **26**
Glastonbury *Som*.............................3D **15**
Glyncoch *Rhon*.................................1A **4**
Glyntaff *Rhon*...................................1A **4**
Goatacre *Wilts*..................................2B **8**
Goathill *Dors*...................................2B **26**
Goathurst *Som*................................3B **14**
Godalming *Surr*..........................2C **23**
Godford Cross *Devn*........................3A **24**
Godmanstone *Dors*.........................1B **36**
Godshill *Hants*................................2C **29**
Godshill *IOW*...................................2C **41**
Goldcliff *Newp*..................................1C **5**
Golden Pot *Hants*............................2A **22**
Gomeldon *Wilts*...............................3C **19**
Gomshall *Surr*.................................2D **23**
Goodworth Clatford *Hants*.............2A **20**
Goose Green *S Glo*............................1C **7**
Goosey *Oxon*...................................1A **10**
Gores *Wilts*......................................1C **19**
Goring *Oxon*....................................1D **11**
Goring-by-Sea *W Sus*......................3D **33**
Goring Heath *Oxon*.........................2D **11**
Gosport *Hants*...........................1D **41**
Graffham *W Sus*..............................2C **33**
Grafham *Surr*..................................2D **23**
Grangetown *Card*.............................2A **4**
Grateley *Hants*................................2D **19**
Grayshott *Hants*.............................3B **22**
Grayswood *Surr*..............................3C **23**
Grazeley *Wok*..................................3D **11**
Great Bedwyn *Wilts*..........................3D **9**
Great Bookham *Surr*.......................1D **23**
Great Chalfield *Wilts*.........................3D **7**
Great Cheverell *Wilts*......................1A **18**
Great Coxwell *Oxon*..........................1D **9**
Great Durnford *Wilts*......................3C **19**
Great Elm *Som*................................2C **17**
Greatham *Hants*.............................3A **22**
Greatham *W Sus*.............................2D **33**
Great Hinton *Wilts*.........................1A **18**
Great Shefford *W Ber*......................2A **10**
Great Shoddesden *Hants*................2D **19**
Great Somerford *Wilts*......................1A **8**
Great Thorness *IOW*........................1B **40**
Great Wishford *Wilts*.......................3B **18**
Green, The *Wilts*..............................3D **17**
Greendown *Som*.............................1A **16**
Greenfield *Oxon*..............................1A **12**
Greenford *G Lon*.........................1D **13**
Greenham *Dors*................................3D **25**
Greenham *Som*................................1A **24**
Greenham *W Ber*.............................3B **10**
Green Ore *Som*................................1A **16**
Greenway *V Glam*..............................2A **4**
Greinton *Som*...................................3D **15**
Greylake *Som*..................................3C **15**
Greywell *Hants*................................1A **22**
Griggs Green *Hants*.........................3B **22**
Grimstone *Dors*...............................1B **36**
Grittenham *Wilts*..............................1B **8**
Grittleton *Wilts*.................................1D **7**
Groes-faen *Rhon*...............................1A **4**
Groes-wen *Cphy*...............................1A **4**
Grove *Dors*......................................3B **36**
Grove *Oxon*.....................................1A **10**
Guildford *Surr*....................**45** (2C **23**)
Gundleton *Hants*.............................3D **21**
Gunville *IOW*...................................2B **40**
Gurnard *IOW*...................................1B **40**
Gurney Slade *Som*...........................2B **16**
Gussage All Saints *Dors*..................2B **28**
Gussage St Andrew *Dors*................2A **28**
Gussage St Michael *Dors*...............2A **28**
Guy's Marsh *Dors*............................1D **27**
Gwaelod-y-garth *Card*......................1A **4**

H

Habin *W Sus*....................................1B **32**
Hale *Hants*......................................2C **29**
Hale *Surr*...2B **22**
Halfway *W Ber*.................................3B **10**
Hallatrow *Bath*................................1B **16**
Hallen *S Glo*......................................1A **6**
Halnaker *W Sus*...............................3C **33**
Halse *Som*.......................................1A **24**
Halstock *Dors*.................................3A **26**
Halsway *Som*...................................3A **14**
Ham *Devn*..3B **24**
Ham *Som*...2B **24**
....(nr Ilminster)
Ham *Som*...1B **24**
....(nr Taunton)
Ham *Som*...1A **24**
....(nr Wellington)
Ham *Wilts*..3A **10**

Hambleden *Buck*.............................1A **12**
Hambledon *Hants*...........................2D **31**
Hambledon *Surr*..............................3C **23**
Hamble-le-Rice *Hants*....................3B **30**
Hambridge *Som*..............................1C **25**
Hambrook *S Glo*................................2B **6**
Hambrook *W Sus*.............................3A **32**
Ham Common *Dors*.........................1D **27**
Ham Green *N Som*............................2A **6**
Hammer *W Sus*................................3B **22**
Hammoon *Dors*...............................2D **27**
Hamp *Som*.......................................3C **15**
Hampreston *Dors*............................1B **38**
Hampstead Norreys *W Ber*.............2C **11**
Hampton *Devn*................................1B **34**
Hampton *G Lon*...............................2D **13**
Hampton *Som*..................................1C **9**
Hamptworth *Wilts*..........................2D **29**
Hamstead *IOW*................................1B **40**
Hamstead Marshall *W Ber*.............3B **10**
Ham Street *Som*..............................3A **16**
Hamworthy *Pool*.............................1A **38**
Hand and Pen *Devn*........................1A **34**
Handy Cross *Buck*...........................1B **12**
Hanford *Dors*..................................2D **27**
Hangersley *Hants*...........................3C **29**
Hanging Langford *Wilts*.................3B **18**
Hangleton *W Sus*............................3D **33**
Hanham *S Glo*...................................2B **6**
Hanham Green *S Glo*.........................2B **6**
Hankerton *Wilts*...............................1A **8**
Hannington *Hants*...........................1C **21**
Hannington *Swin*..............................1C **9**
Hanworth *G Lon*..............................2D **13**
Harbridge *Hants*.............................2C **29**
Harcombe *Devn*...............................1A **34**
Harcombe Bottom *Devn*..................1C **35**
Hardenhuish *Wilts*...........................2A **8**
Hardham *W Sus*...............................2D **33**
Hardington *Som*..............................1C **17**
Hardington Mandeville *Som*..........2A **26**
Hardington Marsh *Som*..................3A **26**
Hardington Moor *Som*....................2A **26**
Hardley *Hants*.................................3B **30**
Hardway *Hants*................................3D **31**
Hardway *Som*...................................3C **17**
Hare *Som*..2B **24**
Harefield *G Lon*...............................1D **13**
Hare Hatch *Wok*..............................2B **12**
Harlington *G Lon*............................2D **13**
Harman's Cross *Dors*......................2A **38**
Harmondsworth *G Lon*...................2D **13**
Harnham *Wilts*.................................1C **29**
Harpford *Devn*................................1A **34**
Harpsden *Oxon*...............................1A **12**
Harrow *G Lon*.............................1D **13**
Harrow on the Hill *G Lon*................1D **13**
Harrow Weald *G Lon*.......................1D **13**
Harry Stoke *S Glo*..............................2B **6**
Hartford Bridge *Hants*...................1A **22**
Hartley Mauditt *Hants*...................3A **22**
Hartley Wespall *Hants*....................1D **21**
Hartley Wintney *Hants*...................1A **22**
Hartswell *Som*.................................1A **24**
Harwell *Oxon*..................................1B **10**
Hascombe *Surr*...............................3C **23**
Haselbury Plucknett *Som*...............2D **25**
Haslemere *Surr*.........................3C **23**
Hatch Beauchamp *Som*..................1C **25**
Hatch End *G Lon*.............................1D **13**
Hatch Green *Som*............................2C **25**
Hatch Warren *Hants*.......................2D **21**
Hatherden *Hants*............................1A **20**
Hattingley *Hants*............................3D **21**
Hatton *G Lon*...................................2D **13**
Havant *Hants*.............................3A **32**
Haven, The *W Sus*...........................3D **23**
Havenstreet *IOW*.............................1C **41**
Havyatt *Som*....................................3A **16**
Hawkchurch *Devn*...........................3C **25**
Hawkeridge *Wilts*...........................1D **17**
Hawkerland *Devn*...........................2A **34**
Hawkesbury *S Glo*.............................1C **7**
Hawkesbury Upton *S Glo*.................1C **7**
Hawkley *Hants*................................1A **32**
Hawley *Hants*..................................1B **22**
Hawthorn Hill *Brac*.........................2B **12**
Haybridge *Som*...............................2A **16**
Haydon *Bath*...................................1B **16**
Haydon *Dors*...................................2B **26**
Haydon *Som*....................................1B **24**
Haydon Wick *Swin*............................1C **9**
Hayes *G Lon*...............................1D **13**
Haylands *IOW*.................................1C **41**
Hayling Island *Hants*...............1A **42**
Hazelbury Bryan *Dors*....................3C **27**
Hazeley *Hants*.................................1A **22**

Headbourne Worthy *Hants*.............3B **20**
Headley *Hants*.................................3B **22**
....(nr Haslemere)
Headley *Hants*.................................3C **11**
....(nr Kingsclere)
Headley Down *Hants*......................3B **22**
Headley Pk. *Bris*................................3A **6**
Heath Common *W Sus*....................2D **33**
Heath End *Hants*............................3C **11**
Heathfield *Som*...............................3A **14**
....(nr Lydeard St Lawrence)
Heathfield *Som*...............................1A **24**
....(nr Norton Fitzwarren)
Heath House *Som*............................2D **15**
Heathrow Airport *G Lon*..................2D **13**
Heathstock *Devn*.............................3B **24**
Heckfield *Hants*...............................3A **12**
Heddington *Wilts*..............................3A **8**
Hedge End *Hants*.......................2B **30**
Hedgerley *Buck*...............................1C **13**
Hedging *Som*...................................1C **25**
Helland *Som*....................................1C **25**
Hemington *Som*..............................1C **17**
Hemsworth *Dors*.............................3A **28**
Hemyock *Devn*.................................2A **24**
Henbury *Bris*.....................................2A **6**
Henfield *S Glo*....................................2B **6**
Henlade *Som*...................................1B **24**
Henley *Dors*....................................3B **26**
Henley *Som*.....................................3D **15**
Henley *W Sus*..................................1B **32**
Henley-on-Thames *Oxon*..........1A **12**
Hensting *Hants*...............................1B **30**
Henstridge *Som*...............................2C **27**
Henstridge Ash *Som*.......................1C **27**
Henstridge Bowden *Som*................1B **26**
Henstridge Marsh *Som*...................1C **27**
Henton *Som*....................................2D **15**
Hermitage *Dors*..............................3B **26**
Hermitage *W Ber*.............................2C **11**
Hermitage *W Sus*............................3A **32**
Herriard *Hants*................................2D **21**
Hersham *Surr*..................................3D **13**
Herston *Dors*...................................3B **38**
Heston *G Lon*...................................2D **13**
Hewish *N Som*...................................3D **5**
Hewish *Som*.....................................3D **25**
Hewood *Dors*...................................3C **25**
Heyshott *W Sus*...............................2B **32**
Heytesbury *Wilts*.............................2A **18**
Heywood *Wilts*................................1D **17**
Highbridge *Som*..............................2C **15**
Highbury *Som*..................................2B **16**
Highclere *Hants*...............................3B **10**
Highcliffe *Dors*.................................1D **39**
High Cross *Hants*............................1A **32**
Higher Alham *Som*..........................2B **16**
Higher Ansty *Dors*...........................3C **27**
Higher Bockhampton *Dors*.............1C **37**
Higher Cheriton *Devn*.....................3A **24**
Higher Halstock Leigh *Dors*............3A **26**
Higher Kingcombe *Dors*.................1A **36**
Higher Melcombe *Dors*...................3C **27**
Higher Nyland *Dors*.........................1C **27**
Higher Tale *Devn*.............................3A **24**
Higher Vexford *Som*........................3A **14**
Higher Whatcombe *Dors*................3D **27**
Higher Wraxall *Dors*........................3A **26**
High Ham *Som*.................................3D **15**
Highleigh *W Sus*..............................1B **42**
High Littleton *Bath*..........................1B **16**
Highmoor *Oxon*...............................1A **12**
Highmoor Cross *Oxon*.....................1A **12**
Highmoor Hill *Mon*...........................1D **5**
High Salvington *W Sus*....................3D **33**
Highstreet Green *Surr*.....................3C **23**
Highworth *Swin*...............................1D **9**
High Wycombe *Buck*..................1B **12**
Hilcott *Wilts*.....................................1C **19**
Hilfield *Dors*....................................3B **26**
Hillbourne *Pool*...............................1B **38**
Hill Brow *Hants*...............................1A **32**
Hillbutts *Dors*..................................3A **28**
Hillcommon *Som*.............................1A **24**
Hill Deverill *Wilts*.............................2D **17**
Hillesley *Glos*.....................................1C **7**
Hillfarrance *Som*.............................1A **24**
Hill Green *W Ber*.............................2B **10**
Hill Head *Hants*..............................3C **31**
Hillingdon *G Lon*.............................1D **13**
Hillstreet *Hants*..............................2A **30**
Hill View *Dors*..................................1A **38**
Hilmarton *Wilts*.................................2B **8**
Hilperton *Wilts*................................1D **17**
Hilperton Marsh *Wilts*....................1D **17**
Hilsea *Port*.......................................3D **31**
Hiltingbury *Hants*...........................1B **30**

Hilton *Dors*.....................................3C 27
Hindhead *Surr*................................3B 22
Hindon *Wilts*..................................3A 18
Hinton *Hants*..................................1D 39
Hinton *S Glo*....................................2C 7
Hinton Ampner *Hants*...................1C 31
Hinton Blewett *Bath*.....................1A 16
Hinton Charterhouse *Bath*............1C 17
Hinton Martell *Dors*......................3B 28
Hinton Parva *Swin*..........................1D 9
Hinton St George *Som*..................2D 25
Hinton St Mary *Dors*......................2C 27
Hipley *Hants*..................................2D 31
Hodson *Swin*....................................1C 9
Hoe Gate *Hants*.............................2D 31
Hogstock *Dors*...............................3A 28
Holbury *Hants*...............................3B 30
Holcombe *Som*...............................2B 16
Holcombe Rogus *Devn*..................2A 24
Holditch *Dors*.................................3C 25
Hole Street *W Sus*.........................2D 33
Holford *Som*...................................2A 14
Holmbury St Mary *Surr*.................2D 23
Holmebridge *Dors*.........................2D 37
Holt *Dors*..3B 28
Holt *Wilts*...3D 7
Holt End *Hants*..............................3D 21
Holt Heath *Dors*............................3B 28
Holton *Som*.....................................1B 26
Holton Heath *Dors*.........................1A 38
Holt Pound *Hants*..........................2B 22
Holwell *Dors*...................................2C 27
Holwell *Som*...................................2C 17
Holworth *Dors*.................................2C 37
Holybourne *Hants*.........................2A 22
Holy City *Devn*...............................3C 25
Holyport *Wind*................................2B 12
Holywell *Dors*.................................3A 26
Holywell *Glos*...................................1C 7
Holywell Lake *Som*........................1A 24
Homington *Wilts*............................1C 29
Honey Street *Wilts*..........................3C 9
Honiton *Devn*.................................3A 24
Hook *Hants*.....................................1A 22
....(nr Basingstoke)
Hook *Hants*.....................................3C 31
....(nr Fareham)
Hook *Wilts*..1B 8
Hooke *Dors*.....................................3A 26
Hordle *Hants*..................................1D 39
Horfield *Bris*.....................................2A 6
Horn Ash *Dors*...............................3C 25
Hornblotton Green *Som*...............3A 16
Horndean *Hants*............................2A 32
Horningsham *Wilts*........................2D 17
Hornsbury *Som*..............................2C 25
Horpit *Swin*.......................................1D 9
Horringford *IOW*.............................2C 41
Horsebridge *Hants*........................3A 20
Horsecastle *N Som*.........................3D 5
Horsell *Surr*.....................................1C 23
Horsey *Som*.....................................3C 15
Horsington *Som*.............................1C 27
Horton *Dors*....................................3B 28
Horton *S Glo*....................................1C 7
Horton *Som*.....................................2C 25
Horton *Wilts*......................................3B 8
Horton *Wind*....................................2D 13
Horton Cross *Som*.........................2C 25
Horton Heath *Hants*.....................2B 30
Houghton *Hants*............................3A 20
Houghton *W Sus*...........................2D 33
Hound *Hants*...................................3B 30
Hound Green *Hants*......................1A 22
Houndsmoor *Som*.........................1A 24
Hounsdown *Hants*.........................2A 30
Hounslow *G Lon*........................2D 13
Howleigh *Som*.................................2B 24
Howley *Som*....................................3B 24
Hoyle *W Sus*...................................2C 33
Huish *Wilts*.......................................3C 9
Huish Champflower *Som*..............1A 24
Huish Episcopi *Som*......................1D 25
Hullavington *Wilts*...........................1D 7
Hulverstone *IOW*............................2A 40
Hundred Acres *Hants*....................2C 31
Hungerford *Hants*.........................2C 29
Hungerford *Som*............................2A 14
Hungerford *W Ber*.........................3A 10
Hungerford Newtown *W Ber*........2A 10
Hunny Hill *IOW*...............................2B 40
Hunston *W Sus*..............................3B 32
Hunstrete *Bath*................................3B 6
Huntham *Som*................................1C 25
Huntingford *Wilts*...........................1D 27
Hunton *Hants*................................3B 20
Huntspill *Som*..................................2C 15

Huntstile *Som*.................................3B 14
Huntworth *Som*...............................3C 15
Hurcot *Som*.....................................1A 26
....(nr Somerton)
Hurcott *Som*....................................2C 25
....(nr Ilminster)
Hurdcott *Wilts*.................................3C 19
Hurley *Wind*.....................................1B 12
Hurn *Dors*.......................................1C 39
Hursey *Dors*....................................3D 25
Hursley *Hants*.................................1B 30
Hurst *Som*.......................................2D 25
Hurst *Wok*.......................................2A 12
Hurstbourne Priors *Hants*.............2B 20
Hurstbourne Tarrant *Hants*..........1A 20
Hurtmore *Surr*................................2C 23
Hutton *N Som*.................................1C 15
Huxham Green *Som*......................3A 16
Hydestile *Surr*.................................2C 23
Hythe *Hants*..............................3B 30
Hythe End *Wind*.............................2D 13

I

Ibberton *Dors*.................................3C 27
Ibsley *Hants*....................................3C 29
Ibstone *Buck*...................................1A 12
Ibthorpe *Hants*...............................1A 20
Ibworth *Hants*................................1C 21
Icelton *N Som*...................................3C 5
Ickenham *G Lon*.............................1D 13
Idmiston *Wilts*.................................3C 19
Idstone *Oxon*....................................1D 9
Ifold *W Sus*.....................................3D 23
Ilchester *Som*.................................1A 26
Ilford *Som*.......................................2C 25
Ilminster *Som*.................................2C 25
Ilsington *Dors*.................................1C 37
Ilton *Som*...2C 25
Imber *Wilts*.....................................2A 18
Inglesbatch *Bath*..............................3C 7
Ingst *S Glo*.......................................1A 6
Inkpen *W Ber*.................................3A 10
Iping *W Sus*....................................1B 32
Ipsden *Oxon*...................................1D 11
Iron Acton *S Glo*..............................1B 6
Isle Abbotts *Som*...........................1C 25
Isle Brewers *Som*..........................1C 25
Isle of Wight *IOW*....................2B 40
Itchen *Sotn*.....................................2B 30
Itchen Abbas *Hants*......................3C 21
Itchenor *W Sus*..............................3A 32
Itchen Stoke *Hants*.......................3C 21
Itchingfield *W Sus*..........................1D 33
Itchington *S Glo*...............................1B 6
Iver Heath *Buck*..............................1D 13
Iwerne Courtney *Dors*...................2D 27
Iwerne Minster *Dors*......................2D 27

J

Jacobs Well *Surr*............................1C 23
Jordans *Buck*..................................1C 13
Jumpers Common *Dors*...............1C 39

K

Keevil *Wilts*.....................................1A 18
Keinton Mandeville *Som*...............3A 16
Kelston *Bath*.....................................3C 7
Kempshott *Hants*..........................2D 21
Kendleshire *S Glo*............................2B 6
Kenn *N Som*.....................................3D 5
Kentisbeare *Devn*..........................3A 24
Kent's Oak *Hants*..........................1A 30
Kersbrook *Devn*.............................2A 34
Kerswell *Devn*................................3A 24
Kewstoke *N Som*.............................3C 5
Keyford *Som*...................................2C 17
Keyhaven *Hants*.............................1A 40
Keynsham *Bath*.........................3B 6
Kidmore End *Oxon*........................2D 11
Kilmersdon *Som*............................1B 16
Kilmeston *Hants*............................1C 31
Kilmington *Devn*............................1B 34
Kilmington *Wilts*.............................3C 17
Kiln Green *Wok*..............................1B 12
Kilton *Som*......................................2A 14
Kilve *Som*..2A 14
Kimmeridge *Dors*...........................3A 38
Kimpton *Hants*...............................2D 19
Kingsbury Episcopi *Som*...............1D 25
Kingsclere *Hants*...........................1C 21
Kingsdon *Som*................................1A 26
Kingsdown *Swin*...............................1C 9
Kingsdown *Wilts*...............................3D 7
Kingsley *Hants*...............................3A 22

Kingsley Green *W Sus*..................3B 22
King's Somborne *Hants*................3A 20
King's Stag *Dors*............................2C 27
Kingston *Dors*.................................2C 27
....(nr Sturminster Newton)
Kingston *Dors*.................................3A 38
....(nr Swanage)
Kingston *Hants*...............................3C 29
Kingston *IOW*..................................2B 40
Kingston *W Sus*..............................3D 33
Kingston Deverill *Wilts*...................3D 17
Kingstone *Som*...............................2C 25
Kingston Lisle *Oxon*.......................1A 10
Kingston Maurward *Dors*..............1C 37
Kingston Russell *Dors*....................1A 36
Kingston St Mary *Som*...................1B 24
Kingston Seymour *N Som*..............3D 5
Kingswood *Glos*................................1C 7
Kingswood *S Glo*........................2B 6
Kingswood *Som*..............................3A 14
Kings Worthy *Hants*.......................3B 20
Kington *S Glo*....................................1B 6
Kington Langley *Wilts*.....................2A 8
Kington Magna *Dors*......................1C 27
Kington St Michael *Wilts*................2A 8
Kingweston *Som*............................3A 16
Kinson *Bour*....................................1B 38
Kintbury *W Ber*..............................3A 10
Kirdford *W Sus*...............................1D 33
Kittisford *Som*.................................1A 24
Kitwood *Hants*................................3D 21
Knaphill *Surr*...................................1C 23
Knapp *Hants*..................................1B 30
Knapp *Som*.....................................1C 25
Knightcott *N Som*...........................1C 15
Knighton *Som*.................................2A 14
Knighton *Dors*................................2B 26
Knighton *Wilts*..................................2D 9
Knockdown *Glos*..............................1D 7
Knole *Som*.......................................1D 25
Knollbury *Mon*..................................1D 5
Knook *Wilts*.....................................2A 18
Knotty Green *Buck*.........................1C 13
Knowle *Devn*...................................2A 34
Knowle *Bris*.......................................2B 6
Knowle St Giles *Som*.....................2C 25
Knowle Village *Hants*....................3C 31
Knowl Hill *Wind*..............................2B 12

L

Lacock *Wilts*.....................................3A 8
Lagness *W Sus*...............................3B 32
Lake *IOW*...2C 41
Lake *Wilts*..3C 19
Laleham *Surr*..................................3D 13
Lambourn *W Ber*............................2A 10
Lambourn Woodlands *W Ber*........2A 10
Lambs Green *Dors*........................1A 38
Lamyatt *Som*..................................3B 16
Landford *Wilts*................................2D 29
Landport *Port*.................................3D 31
Lane End *Buck*...............................1B 12
Lane End *Hants*.............................1C 31
Lane End *IOW*.................................2D 41
Lane End *Wilts*................................2D 17
Langdown *Hants*............................3B 30
Langford *Som*.................................1B 24
Langford Budville *Som*..................1A 24
Langham *Dors*................................1C 27
Langley *Hants*.................................3B 30
Langley *Slo*......................................2D 13
Langley *Som*...................................1A 24
Langley *W Sus*................................1B 32
Langley Burrell *Wilts*.......................2A 8
Langley Marsh *Som*.......................1A 24
Langport *Som*.................................1D 25
Langridge *Bath*................................3C 7
Langrish *Hants*...............................1A 32
Langstone *Hants*............................3A 32
Langton Herring *Dors*....................2B 36
Langton Long Blandford *Dors*.......3D 27
Langton Matravers *Dors*...............3A 38
Lansdown *Bath*................................3C 7
Larkhall *Bath*....................................3C 7
Larkhill *Wilts*...................................2C 19
Lasham *Hants*................................2D 21
Latchmere Green *Hants*................1D 21
Latteridge *S Glo*..............................1B 6
Lattiford *Som*..................................1B 26
Launcherley *Som*...........................2A 16
Laverstock *Wilts*.............................3C 19
Laverstoke *Hants*...........................2B 20
Laverton *Som*.................................1C 17
Laymore *Dors*.................................3C 25
Layter's Green *Buck*......................1C 13
Lea *Wilts*...1A 8

Leckford *Hants*...............................3A 20
Leckhampstead *W Ber*..................2B 10
Leckwith *V Glam*..............................2A 4
Lee *Hants*.......................................2A 30
Leechpool *Mon*................................1A 6
Lee-on-the-Solent *Hants*..............3C 31
Leigh *Dors*......................................3B 26
Leigh *Wilts*..1B 8
Leigh Common *Som*......................1C 27
Leigh Delamere *Wilts*.....................2D 7
Leigh-on-Mendip *Som*...................2B 16
Leigh Pk. *Hants*.............................3A 32
Leighterton *Glos*..............................1D 7
Leighton *Som*.................................2C 17
Lepe *Hants*.....................................1B 40
Letcombe Bassett *Oxon*................1A 10
Letcombe Regis *Oxon*...................1A 10
Leverton *W Ber*..............................2A 10
Lickfold *W Sus*................................1C 33
Liddington *Swin*................................1D 9
Lidsey *W Sus*..................................3C 33
Lightwater *Surr*..............................3C 13
Lillesdon *Som*.................................1C 25
Lillington *Dors*................................2B 26
Lilstock *Som*....................................2A 14
Limington *Som*................................1A 26
Limpley Stoke *Wilts*.........................3C 7
Linchmere *W Sus*..........................3B 22
Lindford *Hants*...............................3B 22
Linford *Hants*..................................3C 29
Linkenholt *Hants*............................1A 20
Linwood *Hants*...............................3C 29
Liphook *Hants*................................3B 22
Lipyeate *Som*..................................1B 16
Lisle Court *Hants*...........................1A 40
Liss *Hants*.......................................1A 32
Liss Forest *Hants*...........................1A 32
Lisvane *Card*....................................1A 4
Liswerry *Newp*..................................1C 5
Litchfield *Hants*..............................1B 20
Little Atherfield *IOW*.......................2B 40
Little Badminton *S Glo*....................1D 7
Little Bedwyn *Wilts*..........................3D 9
Little Bognor *W Sus*.......................1D 33
Little Bookham *Surr*.......................1D 23
Littlebredy *Dors*.............................2A 36
Little Canford *Dors*........................1B 38
Little Cheverell *Wilts*......................1A 18
Littlecott *Wilts*................................1C 19
Little Coxwell *Oxon*.........................1D 9
Little Down *Hants*..........................1A 20
Little Elm *Som*................................2C 17
Littlehampton *W Sus*................3D 33
Little Langford *Wilts*.......................3B 18
Little London *Hants*.......................2A 20
....(nr Andover)
Little London *Hants*.......................1D 21
....(nr Basingstoke)
Little Marlow *Buck*.........................1B 12
Littlemoor *Dors*..............................2B 36
Little Posbrook *Hants*....................3C 31
Little Sandhurst *Brac*....................3B 12
Little Shoddesden *Hants*...............2D 19
Little Sodbury *S Glo*........................1C 7
Little Somborne *Hants*..................3A 20
Little Somerford *Wilts*......................1A 8
Littleton *Surr*...................................2C 23
....(nr Guildford)
Littleton *Surr*...................................3D 13
....(nr Staines)
Littleton *Hants*................................3B 20
Littleton *Som*..................................3D 15
Littleton Drew *Wilts*.........................1D 7
Littleton Pannell *Wilts*....................1B 18
Littleton-upon-Severn *S Glo*..........1A 6
Littlewick Green *Wind*...................2B 12
Littlewindsor *Dors*.........................3D 25
Little Wittenham *Oxon*...................1C 11
Litton *Som*......................................1A 16
Litton Cheney *Dors*.......................1A 36
Llanbeder *Newp*..............................1C 5
Llanbradach *Cphy*............................1A 4
Llancarfan *V Glam*...........................2A 4
Llandaff *Card*....................................2A 4
Llandevaud *Newp*............................1D 5
Llandevenny *Mon*............................1D 5
Llandough *V Glam*...........................2A 4
Llanedeyrn *Card*..............................1B 4
Llanfihangel near Rogiet *Mon*........1D 5
Llanfrechfa *Torf*................................1C 5
Llanhennock *Mon*............................1C 5
Llanishen *Card*.................................1A 4
Llanmartin *Newp*..............................1C 5
Llanrumney *Card*.............................1B 4
Llantarnam *Torf*................................1C 5
Llantrisant *Rhon*..............................1A 4
Llantrithyd *V Glam*...........................2A 4

Llantwit Fardre *Rhon* 1A **4**
Llanvaches *Newp* 1D **5**
Llanvair Discoed *Mon* 1D **5**
Llanwern *Newp* 1C **5**
Lockeridge *Wilts* 3C **9**
Lockerley *Hants* 1D **29**
Locking *N Som* 1C **15**
Locksgreen *IOW* 1B **40**
Locks Heath *Hants* 3C **31**
Loders *Dors* 1D **35**
Lodsworth *W Sus* 1C **33**
London Heathrow Airport *G Lon* ..**48** (2D **13**)
Long Ashton *N Som* 2A **6**
Long Bredy *Dors* 1A **36**
Longbridge Deverill *Wilts* 2D **17**
Longburton *Dors* 2B **26**
Long Common *Hants* 2C **31**
Longcot *Oxon* 1D **9**
Long Crichel *Dors* 2A **28**
Longcross *Surr* 3C **13**
Longford *G Lon* 2D **13**
Longham *Dors* 1B **38**
Longhedge *Wilts* 2D **17**
Longlane *W Ber* 2B **10**
Long Load *Som* 1D **25**
Longmoor Camp *Hants* 3A **22**
Long Newnton *Glos* 1A **8**
Longparish *Hants* 2B **20**
Longstock *Hants* 3A **20**
Longstreet *Wilts* 1C **19**
Long Sutton *Hants* 2A **22**
Long Sutton *Som* 1D **25**
Long Wittenham *Oxon* 1C **11**
Lopcombe Corner *Wilts* 3D **19**
Lopen *Som* 2D **25**
Lordington *W Sus* 3A **32**
Loscombe *Dors* 1A **36**
Lottisham *Som* 3A **16**
Loudwater *Buck* 1C **13**
Lovedean *Hants* 2D **31**
Lover *Wilts* 1D **29**
Lovington *Som* 3A **16**
Lower Ansty *Dors* 3C **27**
Lower Assendon *Oxon* 1A **12**
Lower Basildon *W Ber* 2D **11**
Lower Bockhampton *Dors* 1C **37**
Lower Bordean *Hants* 1D **31**
Lower Bullington *Hants* 2B **20**
Lower Burgate *Hants* 2C **29**
Lower Cheriton *Devn* 3A **24**
Lower Chicksgrove *Wilts* 3A **18**
Lower Chute *Wilts* 1A **20**
Lower Common *Hants* 2D **21**
Lower Everleigh *Wilts* 1C **19**
Lower Eype *Dors* 1D **35**
Lower Failand *N Som* 2A **6**
Lower Farringdon *Hants* 3A **22**
Lower Froyle *Hants* 2A **22**
Lower Godney *Som* 2D **15**
Lower Green *W Ber* 3A **10**
Lower Holditch *Dors* 3C **25**
Lower Horncroft *W Sus* 2D **33**
Lower Kilcott *Glos* 1C **7**
Lower Kingcombe *Dors* 1A **36**
Lower Langford *N Som* 3D **5**
Lower Machen *Newp* 1B **4**
Lower Morton *S Glo* 1B **6**
Lower Nyland *Dors* 1C **27**
Lower Penarth *V Glam* 3A **4**
Lower Pennington *Hants* 1A **40**
Lower Seagry *Wilts* 1A **8**
Lower Shiplake *Oxon* 2A **12**
Lower Stanton St Quintin *Wilts* 1A **8**
Lower Swanwick *Hants* 3B **30**
Lower Tale *Devn* 3A **24**
Lower Upham *Hants* 2C **31**
Lower Vexford *Som* 3A **14**
Lower Weare *Som* 1D **15**
Lower Whatcombe *Dors* 3D **27**
Lower Wield *Hants* 2D **21**
Lower Woodend *Buck* 1B **12**
Lower Woodford *Wilts* 3C **19**
Lower Wraxall *Dors* 3A **26**
Lowford *Hants* 2B **30**
Low Ham *Som* 1D **25**
Lowton *Som* 2A **24**
Loxhill *Surr* 3D **23**
Loxton *N Som* 1C **15**
Loxwood *W Sus* 3D **23**
Luccombe Village *IOW* 2C **41**
Luckington *Wilts* 1D **7**
Ludgershall *Wilts* 1D **19**
Ludwell *Wilts* 1A **28**
Lullington *Som* 1C **17**
Lulsgate Bottom *N Som* 3A **6**
Lulworth Camp *Dors* 2D **37**
Luppitt *Devn* 3A **24**

Lurgashall *W Sus* 1C **33**
Luton *Devn* 3A **24**
Lydeard St Lawrence *Som* 3A **14**
Lyde Green *Hants* 1A **22**
Lydford Fair Place *Som* 3A **16**
Lydiard Millicent *Wilts* 1B **8**
Lydlinch *Dors* 2C **27**
Lydmarsh *Som* 3C **25**
Lyme Regis *Dors* 1C **35**
Lymington *Hants* 1A **40**
Lyminster *W Sus* 3D **33**
Lymore *Hants* 1D **39**
Lympsham *Som* 1C **15**
Lyndhurst *Hants* 3A **30**
Lyne *Surr* 3D **13**
Lyneham *Wilts* 2B **8**
Lyon's Gate *Dors* 3B **26**
Lytchett Matravers *Dors* 1A **38**
Lytchett Minster *Dors* 1A **38**

M

Machen *Cphy* 1B **4**
Maddington *Wilts* 2B **18**
Madehurst *W Sus* 2C **33**
Madford *Devn* 2A **24**
Maes Awyr Caerdydd *V Glam* 3A **4**
Magor *Mon* 1D **5**
Magwyr *Mon* 1D **5**
Maiden Bradley *Wilts* 3D **17**
Maidenhayne *Devn* 1B **34**
Maidenhead *Wind* 1B **12**
Maiden Newton *Dors* 1A **36**
Maiden's Green *Brac* 2B **12**
Maidensgrove *Oxon* 1A **12**
Maindee *Newp* 1C **5**
Malmesbury *Wilts* 1A **8**
Malpas *Newp* 1C **5**
Mangotsfield *S Glo* 2B **6**
Manningford Bohune *Wilts* 1C **19**
Manningford Bruce *Wilts* 1C **19**
Mannington *Dors* 3B **28**
Manston *Dors* 2D **27**
Manswood *Dors* 3A **28**
Manton *Wilts* 3C **9**
Maperton *Som* 1B **26**
Maple Cross *Herts* 1D **13**
Mapledurham *Oxon* 2D **11**
Mapledurwell *Hants* 1D **21**
Mapperton *Dors* 1A **36**
..........(nr Beaminster)
Mapperton *Dors* 1A **38**
..........(nr Poole)
Mappowder *Dors* 3C **27**
Marchwood *Hants* 2A **30**
Marden *Wilts* 1B **18**
Marehill *W Sus* 2D **33**
Margaret Marsh *Dors* 2D **27**
Mark *Som* 2C **15**
Mark Causeway *Som* 2C **15**
Market Lavington *Wilts* 1B **18**
Marksbury *Bath* 3B **6**
Mark's Corner *IOW* 1B **40**
Marlborough *Wilts* 3C **9**
Marlow *Buck* 1B **12**
Marlow Bottom *Buck* 1B **12**
Marlow Common *Buck* 1B **12**
Marnhull *Dors* 2C **27**
Marsh *Devn* 2B **24**
Marshalsea *Dors* 3C **25**
Marsh Benham *W Ber* 3B **10**
Marshfield *Newp* 1B **4**
Marshfield *S Glo* 2C **7**
Marsh Green *Devn* 1A **34**
Marshwood *Dors* 1C **35**
Marston *Wilts* 1A **18**
Marston Magna *Som* 1A **26**
Marten *Wilts* 1D **19**
Martin *Hants* 2B **28**
Martin Drove End *Hants* 1B **28**
Martinstown *Dors* 2B **36**
Martock *Som* 3D **25**
Martyr's Green *Surr* 1D **23**
Martyr Worthy *Hants* 3C **21**
Mathern *Mon* 1A **6**
Mattingley *Hants* 1A **22**
Maybush *Sotn* 2A **30**
Mayes Green *Surr* 3D **23**
Mayford *Surr* 1C **23**
Meadgate *Bath* 1B **16**
Meare *Som* 2D **15**
Meare Green *Som* 1B **24**
..........(nr Curry Mallet)
Meare Green *Som* 1C **25**
..........(nr Stoke St Gregory)
Medmenham *Buck* 1B **12**
Medstead *Hants* 3D **21**

Melbury Abbas *Dors* 1D **27**
Melbury Bubb *Dors* 3A **26**
Melbury Osmond *Dors* 3A **26**
Melbury Sampford *Dors* 3A **26**
Melcombe Bingham *Dors* 3C **27**
Melcombe Regis *Dors* 2B **36**
Melksham *Wilts* 3A **8**
Mells *Som* 2C **17**
Melplash *Dors* 1D **35**
Membury *Devn* 3B **24**
Meon *Hants* 3C **31**
Meonstoke *Hants* 1D **31**
Mere *Wilts* 3D **17**
Merley *Pool* 1B **38**
Merridge *Som* 3B **14**
Merriott *Som* 2D **25**
Merrow *Surr* 1D **23**
Merston *W Sus* 3B **32**
Merstone *IOW* 2C **41**
Merthyr Dyfan *V Glam* 2A **4**
Metcombe *Devn* 1A **34**
Michaelston-le-Pit *V Glam* 2A **4**
Michaelston-y-Fedw *Newp* 1B **4**
Micheldever *Hants* 3C **21**
Michelmersh *Hants* 1A **30**
Middle Assendon *Oxon* 1A **12**
Middle Chinnock *Som* 2D **25**
Middlemarsh *Dors* 3B **26**
Middle Stoughton *Som* 2D **15**
Middleton *Hants* 2B **20**
Middleton *IOW* 2A **40**
Middleton-on-Sea *W Sus* 3C **33**
Middle Wallop *Hants* 3D **19**
Middle Winterslow *Wilts* 3D **19**
Middle Woodford *Wilts* 3C **19**
Middlezoy *Som* 3C **15**
Midelney *Som* 1D **25**
Midford *Bath* 3C **7**
Midgham *W Ber* 3C **11**
Midhurst *W Sus* 1B **32**
Mid Lambrook *Som* 2D **25**
Mid Lavant *W Sus* 3B **32**
Midney *Som* 1A **26**
Midsomer Norton *Bath* 1B **16**
Milborne Port *Som* 2B **26**
Milborne St Andrew *Dors* 1D **37**
Milborne Wick *Som* 1B **26**
Milbourne *Wilts* 1A **8**
Milbury Heath *S Glo* 1B **6**
Mildenhall *Wilts* 3D **9**
Milford *Surr* 2C **23**
Milford on Sea *Hants* 1D **39**
Milkwell *Wilts* 1A **28**
Milland *W Sus* 1B **32**
Millbridge *Surr* 2B **22**
Millbrook *Sotn* 2A **30**
Mill End *Buck* 1A **12**
Millhayes *Devn* 2B **24**
..........(nr Honiton)
Millhayes *Devn* 2A **24**
..........(nr Wellington)
Mill Lane *Hants* 1A **22**
Milston *Wilts* 2C **19**
Milton *Oxon* 1B **10**
Milton *N Som* 3C **5**
Milton *Port* 1D **41**
Milton *Som* 1D **25**
Milton Abbas *Dors* 3D **27**
Milton Clevedon *Som* 3B **16**
Milton Hill *Oxon* 1B **10**
Milton Lilbourne *Wilts* 3C **9**
Milton on Stour *Dors* 1C **27**
Milverton *Som* 1A **24**
Mimbridge *Surr* 3C **13**
Minchington *Dors* 2A **28**
Minety *Wilts* 1B **8**
Minstead *Hants* 2D **29**
Minsted *W Sus* 1B **32**
Minterne Magna *Dors* 3B **26**
Minterne Parva *Dors* 3B **26**
Miskin *Rhon* 1A **4**
Misterton *Som* 3D **25**
Mockbeggar *Hants* 3C **29**
Moneyrow Green *Wind* 2B **12**
Monk Sherborne *Hants* 1D **21**
Monksilver *Som* 3A **14**
Monkton *Devn* 3A **24**
Monkton Combe *Bath* 3C **7**
Monkton Deverill *Wilts* 3D **17**
Monkton Farleigh *Wilts* 3D **7**
Monkton Heathfield *Som* 1B **24**
Monkton Up Wimborne *Dors* 2B **28**
Monkton Wyld *Dors* 1C **35**
Monkwood *Dors* 1D **35**
Monkwood *Hants* 3D **21**
Montacute *Som* 2D **25**
Monxton *Hants* 2A **20**

Moor *Som* 2D **25**
Moorbath *Dors* 1D **35**
Moor Crichel *Dors* 3A **28**
Moordown *Bour* 1B **38**
Moor Green *Wilts* 3D **7**
Moorgreen *Hants* 2B **30**
Moorland *Som* 3C **15**
Moorlinch *Som* 3D **15**
Moorside *Dors* 2C **27**
Moortown *Hants* 3C **29**
Moortown *IOW* 2B **40**
Morcombelake *Dors* 1D **35**
Morestead *Hants* 1C **31**
Moreton *Dors* 2D **37**
Morganstown *Card* 1A **4**
Morgan's Vale *Wilts* 1C **29**
Mortimer *W Ber* 3D **11**
Mortimer West End *Hants* 3D **11**
Morton *S Glo* 1B **6**
Mosterton *Dors* 3D **25**
Motcombe *Dors* 1D **27**
Mottisfont *Hants* 1A **30**
Mottistone *IOW* 2B **40**
Moulsford *Oxon* 1C **11**
Moulton *V Glam* 2A **4**
Mounton *Mon* 1A **6**
Mount Pleasant *Hants* 1D **39**
Muchelney *Som* 1D **25**
Muchelney Ham *Som* 1D **25**
Muckleford *Dors* 1B **36**
Mudeford *Dors* 1C **39**
Mudford *Som* 2A **26**
Mudgley *Som* 2D **15**
Murrell Green *Hants* 1A **22**
Musbury *Devn* 1B **34**
Mynyddislwyn *Cphy* 1A **4**
Mytchett *Surr* 1B **22**

N

Nailsbourne *Som* 1B **24**
Nailsea *N Som* 2D **5**
Nantgarw *Rhon* 1A **4**
Nash *Newp* 1C **5**
Nately Scures *Hants* 1A **22**
Neacroft *Hants* 1C **39**
Nempnett Thrubwell *Bath* 3A **6**
Neston *Wilts* 3D **7**
Netheravon *Wilts* 2C **19**
Netherbury *Dors* 1D **35**
Nether Cerne *Dors* 1B **36**
Nether Compton *Dors* 2A **26**
Netherhampton *Wilts* 1C **29**
Nether Stowey *Som* 3A **14**
Netherstreet *Wilts* 3A **8**
Netherton *Hants* 1A **20**
Nether Wallop *Hants* 3A **20**
Netley Abbey *Hants* 3B **30**
Netley Marsh *Hants* 2A **30**
Nettlebed *Oxon* 1A **12**
Nettlebridge *Som* 2B **16**
Nettlecombe *Dors* 1A **36**
Nettlecombe *IOW* 3C **41**
Nettlestone *IOW* 1D **41**
Nettleton *Wilts* 2D **7**
Netton *Wilts* 3C **19**
New Alresford *Hants* 3C **21**
Newbridge *Hants* 2D **29**
Newbridge *IOW* 2B **40**
New Brighton *Hants* 3A **32**
Newbury *W Ber* 3B **10**
Newbury *Wilts* 2D **17**
New Cheriton *Hants* 1C **31**
Newchurch *IOW* 2C **41**
Newcott *Devn* 3B **24**
New Cross *Som* 2D **25**
New Denham *Buck* 1D **13**
Newell Green *Brac* 2B **12**
Newfound *Hants* 1C **21**
New Haw *Surr* 3D **13**
New Mill *Wilts* 3C **9**
New Milton *Hants* 1D **39**
Newnham *Hants* 1A **22**
Newport *Som* 1C **25**
Newport *IOW* 2C **41**
Newport *Newp* 1C **5**
Newpound Common *W Sus* 1D **33**
New Swanage *Dors* 2B **38**
Newton *Dors* 2C **27**
Newton *Som* 3A **14**
Newton *Wilts* 1D **29**
Newton Green *Mon* 1A **6**
Newton Poppleford *Devn* 2A **34**
Newton St Loe *Bath* 3C **7**
Newton Stacey *Hants* 2B **20**
Newton Toney *Wilts* 2D **19**
Newton Tony *Wilts* 2D **19**

Newton Valence Hants.....................3A 22
New Town Dors.............................2A 28
Newtown Dors...............................3D 25
Newtown Hants.............................2C 31
..............................(nr Bishop's Waltham)
Newtown Hants.............................3B 22
....(nr Liphook)
Newtown Hants.............................2D 29
....(nr Lyndhurst)
Newtown Hants.............................3B 10
....(nr Newbury)
Newtown Hants.............................1A 30
....(nr Romsey)
Newtown Hants.............................3B 30
....(nr Warsash)
Newtown Hants.............................2D 31
....(nr Wickham)
Newtown IOW...............................1B 40
Newtown Pool...............................1B 38
Newtown Som...............................2B 24
Newtown Wilts..............................1A 28
Newyears Green G Lon...................1D 13
Nicholashayne Devn......................2A 24
Nimmer Som................................2C 25
Nine Elms Swin..............................1C 9
Ningwood IOW.............................2B 40
Niton IOW....................................3C 41
Nomansland Wilts.........................2D 29
Norleywood Hants.........................1A 40
Normandy Surr.............................1C 23
Norman's Green Devn.....................3A 24
Norrington Common Wilts...............3D 7
Northam Sotn...............................2B 30
North Ascot Brac...........................3C 13
Northay Som.................................2B 24
North Baddesley Hants...................1A 30
North Barrow Som..........................1B 26
North Bersted W Sus......................3C 33
North Boarhunt Hants....................2D 31
North Bockhampton Dors................1C 39
Northbourne Oxon.........................1C 11
North Bowood Dors.......................1D 35
North Bradley Wilts........................1D 17
North Brewham Som.......................3C 17
North Cadbury Som........................1B 26
Northchapel W Sus.........................1C 33
North Charford Hants.....................2C 29
North Cheriton Som........................1B 26
North Chideock Dors......................1D 35
North Coker Som............................2A 26
Northcott Devn..............................2A 24
North Curry Som............................1C 25
North End Hants.............................3B 10
North End N Som..............................3D 5
North End Port...............................3D 31
North End W Sus............................3D 33
Northend Buck...............................1A 12
Northfield Som...............................3B 14
North Gorley Hants.........................2C 29
North Hayling Hants.......................3A 32
North Heath W Sus.........................1D 33
Northington Hants..........................3C 21
Northleigh Devn.............................1A 34
North Marden W Sus.......................2B 32
Northmoor Green Som....................3C 15
North Moreton Oxon......................1C 11
North Mundham W Sus...................3B 32
North Newnton Wilts......................1C 19
North Newton Som.........................3B 14
Northney Hants..............................3A 32
North Oakley Hants........................1C 21
Northolt G Lon...............................1D 13
Northover Som..............................3D 15
....(nr Glastonbury)
Northover Som..............................1A 26
....(nr Yeovil)
North Perrott Som..........................3D 25
North Petherton Som......................3B 14
North Poorton Dors........................1A 36
Northport Dors..............................2A 38
North Stoke Bath..............................3C 7
North Stoke Oxon...........................1D 11
North Stoke W Sus.........................2D 33
North Street Hants.........................3D 21
North Street W Ber.........................2D 11
North Tidworth Wilts......................2D 19
North Waltham Hants.....................2C 21
North Warnborough Hants..............1A 22
North Weston N Som........................2D 5
North Wick Bath...............................3A 6
Northwick S Glo...............................1A 6
Northwick Som..............................2C 15
North Widcombe Bath....................1A 16
Northwood G Lon...........................1D 13
Northwood IOW.............................1B 40
North Wootton Dors.......................2B 26
North Wootton Som........................2A 16

North Wraxall Wilts..........................2D 7
North Wroughton Swin.....................1C 9
Norton W Sus................................1B 42
....(nr Selsey)
Norton W Sus................................3C 33
....(nr Westergate)
Norton IOW...................................2A 40
Norton Wilts...................................1D 7
Norton Bavant Wilts.......................2A 18
Norton Ferris Wilts.........................3C 17
Norton Fitzwarren Som...................1B 24
Norton Green IOW..........................2A 40
Norton Hawkfield Bath.....................3A 6
Norton Malreward Bath....................3B 6
Norton St Philip Som.......................1C 17
Norton sub Hamdon Som................2D 25
Norwood Pk. Som..........................3A 16
Nottington Dors.............................2B 36
Notton Dors..................................1B 36
Notton Wilts....................................3A 8
Nuffield Oxon................................1D 11
Nunney Som.................................2C 17
Nunton Wilts.................................1C 29
Nursling Hants...............................2A 30
Nursted Hants................................1A 32
Nursteed Wilts.................................3B 8
Nurston V Glam................................3A 4
Nutbourne W Sus..........................3A 32
..................................(nr Chichester)
Nutbourne W Sus..........................2D 33
.................................(nr Pulborough)
Nyetimber W Sus...........................1B 42
Nyewood W Sus.............................1B 32
Nynehead Som..............................1A 24
Nyton W Sus.................................3C 33

O

Oakdale Pool................................1B 38
Oake Som......................................1A 24
Oakhanger Hants...........................3A 22
Oakhill Som...................................2B 16
Oakley Hants.................................1C 21
Oakley Green Wind.........................2C 13
Oaksey Wilts....................................1A 8
Oakshott Hants..............................1A 32
Oakwoodhill Surr...........................3D 23
Oare W Ber...................................2C 11
Oare Wilts..3C 9
Oath Som......................................1C 25
Oborne Dors.................................2B 26
Ockham Surr.................................1D 23
Ockley Surr...................................2D 23
Odcombe Som...............................2A 26
Odd Down Bath................................3C 7
Odiham Hants................................1A 22
Odstock Wilts.................................1C 29
Offham W Sus...............................3D 33
Offwell Devn.................................1A 34
Ogbourne Maizey Wilts...................2C 9
Ogbourne St Andrew Wilts...............2C 9
Ogbourne St George Wilts................2D 9
Okeford Fitzpaine Dors...................2D 27
Okus Swin.......................................1C 9
Old Alresford Hants........................3C 21
Old Basing Hants...........................1D 21
Old Burghclere Hants.....................1B 20
Oldbury-on-Severn S Glo.................1B 6
Oldbury on the Hill Glos...................1D 7
Old Dilton Wilts.............................2D 17
Old Down S Glo...............................1B 6
Oldford Dors.................................1C 17
Oldland S Glo...................................2B 6
Oldmixon N Som............................1C 15
Old Sodbury S Glo............................1C 7
Old Windsor Wind..........................2C 13
Old Woking Surr............................1D 23
Oliver's Battery Hants.....................1B 30
Olveston S Glo.................................1B 6
Onslow Village Surr........................2C 23
Orchard Portman Som....................1B 24
Orcheston Wilts.............................2B 18
Organford Dors..............................1A 38
Osmington Dors............................2C 37
Osmington Mills Dors.....................2C 37
Osterley G Lon...............................2D 13
Othery Som.....................................3C 15
Otterbourne Hants.........................1B 30
Otterford Som...............................2B 24
Otterhampton Som.........................2B 14
Otterton Devn................................2A 34
Ottershaw Surr..............................3D 13
Otterwood Hants............................3B 30
Ottery St Mary Devn.......................1A 34
Outwick Hants...............................2C 29
Over S Glo.......................................1A 6
Overcombe Dors............................2B 36

Over Compton Dors........................2A 26
Overleigh Som...............................3D 15
Over Stowey Som...........................3A 14
Over Stratton Som..........................2D 25
Over Street Wilts............................3B 18
Overton Hants...............................2C 21
Overtown Swin................................2C 9
Over Wallop Hants..........................3D 19
Oving W Sus.................................3C 33
Ovington Hants..............................3C 21
Ower Hants...................................3B 30
....(nr Holbury)
Ower Hants...................................2A 30
....(nr Totton)
Owermoigne Dors.........................2C 37
Owlsmoor Brac.............................3B 12
Ownham W Ber............................2B 10
Owslebury Hants...........................1C 31
Oxbridge Dors...............................1D 35
Oxenpill Som.................................2D 15
Oxenwood Wilts............................1A 20
Oxshott Surr.................................3D 13
Ozleworth Glos................................1C 7

P

Packers Hill Dors............................2C 27
Padworth W Ber...........................3D 11
Pagham W Sus..............................1B 42
Palestine Hants.............................2D 19
Paley Street Wind..........................2B 12
Pallington Dors.............................1C 37
Palmerstown V Glam........................3A 4
Pamber End Hants.........................1D 21
Pamber Green Hants......................1D 21
Pamber Heath Hants......................3D 11
Pamphill Dors................................3A 28
Panborough Som..........................2D 15
Pangbourne W Ber.........................2D 11
Parbrook Som...............................3A 16
Parbrook W Sus.............................1D 33
Parc-Seymour Newp........................1D 5
Pardown Hants.............................2C 21
Park Corner Oxon..........................1D 11
Park Gate Hants............................3C 31
Parkhurst IOW..............................1B 40
Parkstone Pool..............................1B 38
Park Street W Sus..........................3D 23
Parley Cross Dors..........................1B 38
Parmoor Buck...............................1A 12
Passfield Hants..............................3B 22
Patching W Sus.............................3D 33
Patchway S Glo................................1B 6
Pathe Som....................................3C 15
Patney Wilts..................................1B 18
Paulton Bath.................................1B 16
Pawlett Som..................................2B 14
Payhembury Devn.........................3A 24
Payton Som...................................1A 24
Peasedown St John Bath................1C 17
Peasemore W Ber..........................2B 10
Peaslake Surr................................2D 23
Peasmarsh Som.............................2C 25
Peasmarsh Surr.............................2C 23
Pedwell Som.................................3D 15
Peel Common Hants.......................3C 31
Penarth V Glam...............................2A 4
Pendomer Som..............................2A 26
Pendoylan V Glam...........................2A 4
Pengam Card...................................2B 4
Penhill Swin....................................1C 9
Penhow Newp................................1D 5
Pen-marc V Glam.............................3A 4
Penmark V Glam..............................3A 4
Penn Buck.....................................1C 13
Penn Dors.....................................1C 35
Pennington Hants..........................1A 40
Pennsylvania S Glo...........................2C 7
Penselwood Som...........................3C 17
Pensford Bath..................................3B 6
Penton Mewsey Hants....................2A 20
Pentre-poeth Newp..........................1B 4
Pentridge Dors..............................2B 28
Pentwyn Card..................................1B 4
Pentyrch Card..................................1A 4
Pen-y-coedcae Rhon........................1A 4
Penyrheol Cphy................................1A 4
Peper Harow Surr..........................2C 23
Perham Down Wilts.......................2D 19
Perry Green Wilts............................1A 8
Perry Street Som............................3C 25
Pertwood Wilts.............................3D 17
Petersfield Hants...........................1A 32
Petersfinger Wilts..........................1C 29
Peterstone Wentlooge Newp............1B 4
Peterston-super-Ely V Glam.............2A 4
Petworth W Sus.............................1C 33

Pewsey Wilts....................................3C 9
Pheasant's Hill Buck.......................1A 12
Phoenix Green Hants......................1A 22
Pibsbury Som................................1D 25
Picket Piece Hants..........................2A 20
Picket Post Hants...........................3C 29
Pict's Hill Som...............................1D 25
Piddlehinton Dors..........................1C 37
Piddletrenthide Dors......................3C 27
Pidney Dors..................................3C 27
Pightley Som.................................3B 14
Pikeshill Hants...............................3D 29
Pilford Dors...................................3B 28
Pill N Som.......................................2A 6
Pill, The Mon...................................1D 5
Pilley Hants...................................1A 40
Pillgrewelly Newp.............................1C 5
Pillwell Dors..................................2C 27
Pilning S Glo....................................1A 6
Pilsdon Dors.................................1D 35
Pilton Som.....................................2A 16
Pimperne Dors..............................3A 28
Pinkneys Green Wind......................1B 12
Pinner G Lon................................1D 13
Pirbright Surr.................................1C 23
Pishill Oxon...................................1A 12
Pitch Place Surr.............................1C 23
Pitcombe Som...............................3B 16
Pitminster Som..............................2B 24
Pitney Som....................................1D 25
Pitsford Hill Som............................3A 14
Pitt Hants.....................................1B 30
Pitton Wilts...................................3D 19
Plainsfield Som..............................3A 14
Plaistow W Sus.............................3D 23
Plaitford Wilts...............................2D 29
Plastow Green Hants......................3C 11
Play Hatch Oxon............................2A 12
Plush Dors....................................3C 27
Plymtree Devn...............................3A 24
Podimore Som...............................1A 26
Pokesdown Bour.............................1C 39
Poling W Sus.................................3D 33
Poling Corner W Sus......................3D 33
Polsham Som.................................2A 16
Pondtail Hants...............................1B 22
Ponthir Torf.....................................1C 5
Pontypridd Rhon.............................1A 4
Pontywaun Cphy..............................1B 4
Pooksgreen Hants.........................2A 30
Poole Pool............................48 (1B 38)
Poole Som.....................................1A 24
Popeswood Brac...........................3B 12
Popham Hants..............................2C 21
Popley Hants.................................1D 21
Porchfield IOW..............................1B 40
Portbury N Som...............................2A 6
Portchester Hants..........................3D 31
Portesham Dors............................2B 36
Portfield Som.................................1D 25
Portherci V Glam.............................3A 4
Porthkerry V Glam...........................3A 4
Portishead N Som............................2D 5
Portmore Hants.............................1A 40
Porton Wilts..................................3C 19
Portsea Port..................................3D 31
Portskewett Mon.............................1A 6
Portsmouth Port................45 (3D 31)
Port Solent Port.............................3D 31
Portswood Sotn.............................2B 30
Post Green Dors.............................1A 38
Potterne Wilts...............................1A 18
Potterne Wick Wilts........................1B 18
Pottle Street Wilts..........................2D 17
Poulner Hants...............................3C 29
Poulshot Wilts................................1A 18
Poundbury Dors.............................1B 36
Pound Street Hants........................3B 10
Powerstock Dors............................1A 36
Poxwell Dors.................................2C 37
Poyle Slo.......................................2D 13
Poyntington Dors...........................1B 26
Prescott Devn................................2A 24
Preshute Wilts..................................3C 9
Prestleigh Som..............................2B 16
Preston Wilts...................................2D 9
....(nr Aldbourne)
Preston Wilts...................................2B 8
....(nr Lyneham)
Preston Som..................................2C 37
Preston Bowyer Som......................1A 24
Preston Candover Hants.................2D 21
Preston Plucknett Som...................2A 26
Priddy Som...................................1A 16
Priestwood Brac............................2B 12
Prinsted W Sus..............................3A 32
Priory, The W Ber...........................3A 10

Priston Bath..........................3B 6
Privett Hants.........................1D 31
Publow Bath..........................3B 6
Puckington Som......................2C 25
Pucklechurch S Glo.................2B 6
Puddletown Dors....................1C 37
Pulborough W Sus...................2D 33
Pulham Dors...........................3C 27
Puncknowle Dors....................2A 36
Puriton Som...........................2C 15
Purley on Thames W Ber..........2D 11
Purse Caundle Dors................2B 26
Purtington Som.......................3C 25
Purton Wilts...........................1B 8
Purton Stoke Wilts..................1B 8
Puttenham Surr......................2C 23
Puxey Dors.............................2C 27
Puxton N Som.........................3D 5
Pwllmeyric Mon......................1A 6
Pye Corner Newp....................1C 5
Pyle IOW................................3B 40
Pyle Hill Surr..........................1C 23
Pylle Som...............................3B 16
Pymore Dors..........................1D 35
Pyrford Surr...........................1D 23
Pyrford Village Surr.................1D 23

Q

Quarley Hants.........................2D 19
Queen Camel Som...................1A 26
Queen Charlton Bath...............3B 6
Queen Oak Dors.....................3C 17
Quemerford Wilts....................3B 8
Quick's Green W Ber...............2C 11
Quidhampton Hants.................1C 21
Quidhampton Wilts..................3C 19

R

Rackham W Sus.......................2D 33
Radford Bath..........................1B 16
Radipole Dors.........................2B 36
Radstock Bath.........................1B 16
Radyr Card.............................1A 4
Ragged Appleshaw Hants.........2A 20
Rake W Sus............................1B 32
Ram Alley Wilts.......................3D 9
Rampisham Dors.....................3A 26
Ramsbury Wilts.......................2D 9
Ramsdean Hants.....................1A 32
Ramsdell Hants.......................1C 21
Ramsnest Common Surr...........3C 23
Rangeworthy S Glo..................1B 6
Ranmore Common Surr............1D 23
Rapps Som.............................2C 25
Ratley Hants...........................1A 30
Rawridge Devn.......................3B 24
Raymond's Hill Devn................1C 35
Rayners Lane G Lon.................1D 13
Reading Read......................46 (2A 12)
Redcliffe Bay N Som................2D 5
Redford W Sus........................1B 32
Redhill N Som.........................3A 6
Redland Bris...........................2A 6
Redlynch Som.........................3C 17
Redlynch Wilts........................1D 29
Redwick Newp........................1D 5
Redwick S Glo........................1A 6
Regil N Som............................3A 6
Remenham Wok......................1A 12
Remenham Hill Wok.................1A 12
Restrop Wilts..........................1B 8
Rew Street IOW.......................1B 40
Reybridge Wilts.......................3A 8
Rhiwbina Card........................1A 4
Rhiwderin Newp......................1B 4
Rhoose V Glam........................3A 4
Y Rhws V Glam........................3A 4
Rhydyfelin Rhon......................1A 4
Richings Pk. Buck....................2D 13
Rickford N Som.......................1D 15
Ridge Dors.............................2A 38
Ridge Wilts.............................3A 18
Rimpton Som..........................1B 26
Ringwood Hants..................3C 29
Ripley Hants...........................1C 39
Ripley Surr.............................1D 23
Risca Cphy.........................1B 4
Riseley Wok...........................3A 12
Rivar Wilts.............................3A 10
River W Sus............................1C 33
Roath Card.............................2A 4
Rock W Sus............................2D 33
Rockbourne Hants...................2C 29
Rockford Hants.......................3C 29

Rockhampton S Glo.................1B 6
Rockley Wilts..........................2C 9
Rockwell End Buck..................1A 12
Rockwell Green Som................2A 24
Rodbourne Wilts.....................1A 8
Rodden Dors...........................2B 36
Rode Som...............................1D 17
Rodney Stoke Som..................2D 15
Rodway Som............................3B 14
Rodwell Dors..........................3B 36
Rogate W Sus.........................1B 32
Rogerstone Newp....................1B 4
Rogiet Mon.............................1D 5
Roke Oxon..............................1D 11
Rokemarsh Oxon......................1D 11
Romford Dors.........................3B 28
Romsey Hants.....................1A 30
Rookley IOW...........................2C 41
Rooks Bridge Som...................1C 15
Rook's Nest Som.....................3A 14
Rookwood W Sus.....................1A 42
Ropley Hants..........................3D 21
Ropley Dean Hants..................3D 21
Rosemary Lane Devn...............2A 24
Rotherfield Greys Oxon............1A 12
Rotherfield Peppard Oxon.........1A 12
Rotherwick Hants....................1A 22
Rotten Row W Ber...................2C 11
Roud IOW...............................2C 41
Roundham Som.......................3D 25
Roundhurst W Sus...................3C 23
Roundstreet Common W Sus.....1D 33
Roundway Wilts......................3B 8
Rousdon Devn........................1B 34
Row Ash Hants.......................2C 31
Rowberrow Som......................1D 15
Rowde Wilts...........................3A 8
Rowhook W Sus......................3D 23
Rowlands Castle Hants............2A 32
Rowledge Hants......................2B 22
Rowly Surr.............................2D 23
Rowner Hants.........................3C 31
Rownhams Hants.....................2A 30
Rowstock Oxon.......................1B 10
Row Town Surr........................3D 13
Royal Wootton Bassett Wilts..1B 8
Royston Water Som..................2B 24
Rudge Wilts............................1D 17
Rudgeway S Glo......................1B 6
Rudgwick W Sus......................3D 23
Rudloe Wilts...........................2D 7
Rudry Cphy............................1B 4
Ruislip G Lon......................1D 13
Ruislip Common G Lon.............1D 13
Rumney Card..........................2B 4
Rumwell Som..........................1A 24
Runcton W Sus........................3B 32
Runfold Surr...........................2B 22
Runnington Som......................1A 24
Ruscombe Wok.......................2A 12
Rushall Wilts..........................1C 19
Rushmoor Surr.......................2B 22
Russell's Water Oxon...............1A 12
Rustington W Sus....................3D 33
Ryall Dors..............................1D 35
Ryde IOW...........................1C 41
Ryme Intrinseca Dors...............2A 26

S

St Andrews Major V Glam.........2A 4
St Bartholomew's Hill Wilts.......1A 28
St Bride's Netherwent Mon.......1D 5
St Bride's-super-Ely V Glam......2A 4
St Brides Wentlooge Newp........1B 4
St Catherine Bath....................2C 7
St Cross Hants........................1B 30
St Edith's Marsh Wilts..............3A 8
St Fagans Card.......................2A 4
St George's N Som..................3C 5
St Georges V Glam..................2A 4
St George's Hill Surr................3D 13
St Giles's Hill Hants................1B 30
St Helens IOW........................2D 41
Saint Hill Devn........................3A 24
St Ives Dors...........................3C 29
St Lawrence IOW.....................3C 41
St Leonards Dors.....................3C 29
St Lythans V Glam...................2A 4
St Margaret's Wilts..................3D 9
St Mary Bourne Hants..............1B 20
St Mellons Card......................1B 4
St Nicholas V Glam..................2A 4
Salcombe Regis Devn..............2A 34
Salisbury Wilts....................46 (3C 19)
Salterton Wilts........................3C 19

Saltford Bath..........................3B 6
Salway Ash Dors.....................1D 35
Sambourne Wilts.....................2D 17
Sampford Arundel Som.............2A 24
Sampford Brett Som................2A 14
Sand Som...............................2D 15
Sandbanks Pool......................2B 38
Sandford Dors........................2A 38
Sandford Hants.......................3C 29
Sandford IOW.........................2C 41
Sandford N Som......................1D 15
Sandford Orcas Dors...............1B 26
Sandhills Surr.........................2B 26
Sandhills Surr.........................3C 23
Sandhurst Brac...................3B 12
Sandleheath Hants..................2C 29
Sandown IOW......................2C 41
Sands, The Surr......................2B 22
Sandy Lane Wilts.....................3A 8
Sarisbury Green Hants.............3C 31
Satwell Oxon..........................1A 12
Sea Som................................2C 25
Seaborough Dors....................3D 25
Seale Surr..............................2B 22
Sea Mills Bris.........................2A 6
Seaton Devn...........................1B 34
Seavington St Mary Som...........2D 25
Seavington St Michael Som.......2D 25
Sedbury Glos..........................1A 6
Sedgehill Wilts........................1D 27
Seend Wilts............................3A 8
Seend Cleeve Wilts..................3A 8
Seer Green Buck.....................1C 13
Segensworth Hants..................3C 31
Selborne Hants.......................3A 22
Selham W Sus.........................1C 33
Sellick's Green Som.................2B 24
Sells Green Wilts....................3A 8
Selsey W Sus..........................1B 42
Semington Wilts......................3D 7
Semley Wilts..........................1D 27
Send Surr..............................1D 23
Send Marsh Surr.....................1D 23
Senghenydd Cphy...................1A 4
Setley Hants...........................3A 30
Seven Ash Som.......................3A 14
Sevenhampton Swin.................1D 9
Severn Beach S Glo.................1A 6
Shackleford Surr.....................2C 23
Shaftesbury Dors....................1D 27
Shaggs Dors...........................2D 37
Shalbourne Wilts.....................3A 10
Shalcombe IOW.......................2A 40
Shalden Hants........................2D 21
Shalfleet IOW..........................2B 40
Shalford Surr..........................2D 23
Shamley Green Surr.................2D 23
Shanklin IOW......................2C 41
Shapwick Dors.......................3A 28
Shapwick Som........................3D 15
Sharcott Wilts.........................1C 19
Sharnhill Green Dors...............3C 27
Shaw W Ber............................3B 10
Shaw Wilts..............................3D 7
Shawford Hants.......................1B 30
Shearston Som........................3B 14
Shedfield Hants......................2C 31
Sheepway N Som....................2D 5
Sheerwater Surr......................3D 13
Sheet Hants...........................1A 32
Sheffield Bottom W Ber............3D 11
Shefford Woodlands W Ber.......2A 10
Sheldon Devn.........................3A 24
Shellingford Oxon....................1A 10
Shepherd's Green Oxon...........1A 12
Shepperton Surr......................3D 13
Shepton Beauchamp Som.........2D 25
Shepton Mallet Som.................2B 16
Shepton Montague Som...........3B 16
Sherborne Dors......................2B 26
Sherborne Causeway Dors........1D 27
Sherborne St John Hants.........1D 21
Shere Surr.............................2D 23
Sherfield English Hants............1D 29
Sherfield on Loddon Hants.......1D 21
Sherford Dors.........................1A 38
Sherrington Wilts....................3A 18
Sherston Wilts........................1D 7
Shide IOW..............................2B 40
Shillingford Oxon.....................1C 11
Shillingstone Dors...................2D 27
Shilvinghampton Dors..............2B 36
Shinfield Wok.........................3A 12

Shipham Som.........................1D 15
Shiplake Oxon........................2A 12
Shipley W Sus........................1D 33
Shipton Bellinger Hants...........2D 19
Shipton Gorge Dors.................1D 35
Shipton Green W Sus...............1B 42
Shipton Moyne Glos.................1D 7
Shirehampton Bris...................2A 6
Shirenewton Mon....................1D 5
Shirley Sotn...........................2A 30
Shirrell Heath Hants................2C 31
Sholing Sotn..........................2B 30
Shoreditch Som......................1B 24
Shortwood S Glo.....................2B 6
Shorwell IOW..........................2B 40
Shoscombe Bath.....................1C 17
Shottermill Surr......................3B 22
Shreding Green Buck...............1D 13
Shrewton Wilts.......................2B 18
Shripney W Sus......................3C 33
Shrivenham Oxon....................1D 9
Shroton Dors..........................2D 27
Shurlock Row Wind.................2B 12
Shurton Som..........................2B 14
Shute Devn............................1B 34
Sid Devn................................2A 34
Sidbury Devn..........................1A 34
Sidcot N Som.........................1D 15
Sidford Devn..........................1A 34
Sidlesham W Sus.....................1B 42
Sidmouth Devn....................2A 34
Silchester Hants.....................3D 11
Sindlesham Wok......................3A 12
Singleton W Sus......................2B 32
Sipson G Lon..........................2D 13
Siston S Glo...........................2B 6
Sixpenny Handley Dors............2A 28
Skirmett Buck.........................1A 12
Slade, The W Ber....................3C 11
Slade End Oxon......................1C 11
Slaughterford Wilts..................2D 7
Sleaford Hants........................3B 22
Slepe Dors.............................1A 38
Slindon W Sus........................3C 33
Slinfold W Sus........................3D 23
Slough Slo.........................2C 13
Slough Green Som...................1B 24
Smallridge Devn......................3C 25
Smannell Hants.......................2A 20
Smeatharpe Devn....................2B 24
Smitham Hill Bath....................1A 16
Smithincott Devn.....................2A 24
Soake Hants...........................2D 31
Soberton Hants.......................2D 31
Soberton Heath Hants..............2D 31
Soldridge Hants......................3D 21
Solent Breezes Hants..............3C 31
Somerford Dors......................1C 39
Somerley W Sus......................1B 42
Somerton Som........................1D 25
Sonning Wok..........................2A 12
Sonning Common Oxon............1A 12
Sonning Eye Oxon...................2A 12
Sopley Hants..........................1C 39
Sopworth Wilts........................1D 7
Soundwell S Glo.....................2B 6
Southall G Lon....................2D 13
South Ambersham W Sus.........1C 33
Southampton Sotn.............46 (2B 30)
Southampton Airport Hants......2B 30
South Ascot Wind....................3C 13
South Baddesley Hants............1A 40
South Barrow Som...................1B 26
South Bersted W Sus...............3C 33
Southbourne Bour....................1C 39
Southbourne W Sus.................3A 32
South Bowood Dors.................1D 35
South Brewham Som................3C 17
South Cadbury Som.................1B 26
South Chard Som.....................3C 25
South Cheriton Som................1B 26
South Common Devn...............3C 25
Southcott Wilts.......................1C 19
Southdown Bath......................3C 7
Southend W Ber......................2C 11
Southerton Devn......................1A 34
South Fawley W Ber.................1A 10
South Gorley Hants..................2C 29
South Harting W Sus................2A 32
South Hayling Hants................1A 42
South Hill Som........................1D 25
Southington Hants...................2C 21
Southleigh Devn......................1B 34
South Marston Swin.................1C 9
South Moreton Oxon................1C 11
South Mundham W Sus............3B 32
South Newton Wilts.................3B 18

South Oxhey *Herts*......................1D **13**
South Perrott *Dors*.....................3D **25**
South Petherton *Som*.................2D **25**
South Poorton *Som*....................1A **36**
Southrope *Hants*........................2D **21**
Southsea *Port*............................1D **41**
South Stoke *Bath*........................3C **7**
South Stoke *Oxon*......................1C **11**
South Stoke *W Sus*....................3D **33**
South Tidworth *Wilts*.................2D **19**
South Town *Hants*......................3D **21**
South Warnborough *Hants*..........2A **22**
Southwater *W Sus*.....................1D **33**
Southway *Som*...........................2A **16**
South Weirs *Hants*.....................3D **29**
Southwell *Dors*..........................3B **36**
Southwick *Hants*........................3D **31**
Southwick *Wilts*........................1D **17**
South Widcombe *Bath*................1A **16**
South Wonston *Hants*.................3B **20**
Southwood *Som*........................3A **16**
South Wraxall *Wilts*....................3D **7**
Sparkford *Som*...........................1B **26**
Sparsholt *Hants*.........................3B **20**
Sparsholt *Oxon*..........................1A **10**
Spaxton *Som*............................3B **14**
Spear Hill *W Sus*.......................2D **33**
Speen *W Ber*............................3B **10**
Spencers Wood *Wok*.................3A **12**
Spetisbury *Dors*........................3A **28**
Spreakley *Surr*..........................2B **22**
Spring Vale *IOW*........................1D **41**
Staines-upon-Thames *Surr*......2D **13**
Stakes *Hants*............................3D **31**
Stalbridge *Dors*.........................2C **27**
Stalbridge Weston *Dors*.............2C **27**
Stallen *Dors*..............................2B **26**
Stanbridge *Dors*........................3B **28**
Standerwick *Som*.......................1D **17**
Standford *Hants*.........................3B **22**
Standon *Hants*...........................1B **30**
Stanford Dingley *W Ber*..............2C **11**
Stanford in the Vale *Oxon*...........1A **10**
Stanmore *Hants*.........................1B **30**
Stanmore *W Ber*........................2B **10**
Stanton Drew *Bath*.....................3A **6**
Stanton Fitzwarren *Swin*..............1C **9**
Stanton Prior *Bath*.....................3B **6**
Stanton St Bernard *Wilts*.............3B **8**
Stanton St Quintin *Wilts*..............2A **8**
Stanton Wick *Bath*.....................3B **6**
Stanwell *Surr*............................2D **13**
Stanwell Moor *Surr*....................2D **13**
Stapehill *Dors*...........................3B **28**
Staple Fitzpaine *Som*..................2B **24**
Stapleford *Wilts*.........................3B **18**
Staplegrove *Som*.......................1B **24**
Staplehay *Som*..........................1B **24**
Staple Hill *S Glo*.........................2B **6**
Staplers *IOW*............................2C **41**
Stapleton *Bris*...........................2B **6**
Stapleton *Som*...........................1D **25**
Stapley *Som*.............................2A **24**
Startley *Wilts*.............................1A **8**
Stathe *Som*..............................1C **25**
Staverton *Wilts*..........................3D **7**
Stawell *Som*.............................3C **15**
Stawley *Som*............................1A **24**
Steart *Som*...............................2B **14**
Stedham *W Sus*........................1B **32**
Steep *Hants*..............................1A **32**
Steeple *Dors*.............................2A **38**
Steeple Ashton *Wilts*..................1A **18**
Steeple Langford *Wilts*................3B **18**
Stembridge *Som*........................1D **25**
Stenhill *Devn*............................2A **24**
Stert *Wilts*................................1B **18**
Steventon *Hants*........................2C **21**
Steventon *Oxon*.........................1B **10**
Stewley *Som*.............................2C **25**
Stibb Green *Wilts*.......................3D **9**
Sticklinch *Som*..........................3A **16**
Stileway *Som*............................2D **15**
Stinsford *Dors*...........................1C **37**
Stitchcombe *Wilts*......................3D **9**
Stoborough *Dors*.......................2A **38**
Stoborough Green *Dors*..............2A **38**
Stockbridge *Hants*.....................3A **20**
Stockcross *W Ber*......................3B **10**
Stockland *Devn*..........................3B **24**
Stockland Bristol *Som*.................2B **14**
Stockley *Wilts*...........................3B **8**
Stocklinch *Som*..........................2C **25**
Stockton *Wilts*..........................3A **18**
Stockwood *Bris*.........................3B **6**
Stoford *Som*.............................2A **26**
Stoford *Wilts*.............................3B **18**

Stogumber *Som*........................3A **14**
Stogursey *Som*..........................2B **14**
Stoke *Hants*..............................1B **20**
....(nr Andover)
Stoke *Hants*..............................3A **32**
.................................(nr South Hayling)
Stoke Abbott *Dors*.....................3D **25**
Stoke Charity *Hants*...................3B **20**
Stoke D'Abernon *Surr*................1D **23**
Stoke Farthing *Wilts*..................1B **28**
Stokeford *Dors*..........................2D **37**
Stoke Gifford *S Glo*.....................2B **6**
Stoke Poges *Buck*......................1C **13**
Stoke Row *Oxon*.........................1D **11**
Stoke St Gregory *Som*................1C **25**
Stoke St Mary *Som*....................1B **24**
Stoke St Michael *Som*................2B **16**
Stoke sub Hamdon *Som*.............2D **25**
Stoke Trister *Som*......................1C **27**
Stoke Wake *Dors*......................3C **27**
Stolford *Som*.............................2B **14**
Stone *Som*...............................3A **16**
Stone Allerton *Som*...................1D **15**
Ston Easton *Som*......................1B **16**
Stoner Hill *Hants*........................1A **32**
Stoney Cross *Hants*...................2D **29**
Stoney Stoke *Som*.....................3C **17**
Stoney Stratton *Som*..................3B **16**
Stonor *Oxon*.............................1A **12**
Stopham *W Sus*........................2D **33**
Storrington *W Sus*......................2D **33**
Stoughton *Surr*..........................1C **23**
Stoughton *W Sus*......................2B **32**
Stourpaine *Dors*........................3D **27**
Stour Provost *Dors*....................1C **27**
Stour Row *Dors*........................1D **27**
Stourton *Wilts*...........................3C **17**
Stourton Caundle *Dors*...............2C **27**
Stowell *Som*.............................1B **26**
Stowey *Bath*.............................1A **16**
Stowford *Devn*..........................2A **34**
Straight Soley *Wilts*....................2A **10**
Stratfield Mortimer *W Ber*...........3D **11**
Stratfield Saye *Hants*..................3D **11**
Stratfield Turgis *Hants*................1D **21**
Stratford sub Castle *Wilts*...........3C **19**
Stratford Tony *Wilts*...................1B **28**
Stratton *Dors*............................1B **36**
Stratton-on-the-Fosse *Som*.........1B **16**
Stratton St Margaret *Swin*...........1C **9**
Stream *Som*.............................3A **14**
Streatley *W Ber*.........................1C **11**
Street *Som*...............................3C **25**
....(nr Chard)
Street *Som*.............................3D **15**
.....................................(nr Glastonbury)
Street Ash *Som*........................2B **24**
Street End *W Sus*......................1B **42**
Street on the Fosse *Som*............3B **16**
Stretcholt *Som*..........................2B **14**
Stringston *Som*..........................2A **14**
Strood Green *W Sus*..................1D **33**
.....................................(nr Billingshurst)
Strood Green *W Sus*..................3D **23**
....(nr Horsham)
Stroud *Hants*............................1A **32**
Stubbington *Hants*...................3C **31**
Stubhampton *Dors*....................2A **28**
Stuckton *Hants*..........................2C **29**
Studland *Dors*...........................2B **38**
Studley *Wilts*............................2A **8**
Sturminster Marshall *Dors*...........3A **28**
Sturminster Newton *Dors*............2C **27**
Sudbrook *Mon*..........................1A **6**
Sulham *W Ber*...........................2D **11**
Sulhamstead *W Ber*...................3D **11**
Sullington *W Sus*.......................2D **33**
Sully *V Glam*.............................3A **4**
Summersdale *W Sus*..................3B **32**
Sunbury *Surr*...........................3D **13**
Sunningdale *Wind*......................3C **13**
Sunninghill *Wind*.......................3C **13**
Sunton *Wilts*.............................1D **19**
Sutton *Buck*..............................2D **13**
Sutton *Som*...............................3B **16**
Sutton *W Sus*...........................2C **33**
Sutton Abinger *Surr*...................2D **23**
Sutton Benger *Wilts*...................2A **8**
Sutton Bingham *Som*.................2A **26**
Sutton Courtenay *Oxon*..............1C **11**
Sutton Green *Surr*.....................1D **23**
Sutton Mallet *Som*.....................3C **15**
Sutton Mandeville *Wilts*..............1A **28**
Sutton Montis *Som*....................1B **26**
Sutton Poyntz *Dors*...................2C **37**

Sutton Scotney *Hants*.................3B **20**
Sutton Veny *Wilts*......................2A **18**
Sutton Waldron *Dors*..................2D **27**
Swainswick *Bath*........................3C **7**
Swallowcliffe *Wilts*.....................1A **28**
Swallowfield *Wok*.......................3A **12**
Swampton *Hants*........................1B **20**
Swanage *Dors*.........................3B **38**
Swanbridge *V Glam*....................3A **4**
Swanmore *Hants*........................2C **31**
Swanwick *Hants*........................3C **31**
Swarraton *Hants*........................3C **21**
Sway *Hants*..............................1D **39**
Swaythling *Sotn*.........................2B **30**
Swell *Som*................................1C **25**
Swindon *Swin*..............47 (1C **9**)
Swineford *S Glo*.........................3B **6**
Swyre *Dors*..............................2A **36**
Sydenham *Som*.........................3C **15**
Sydling St Nicholas *Dors*............1B **36**
Sydmonton *Hants*......................1B **20**
Symondsbury *Dors*....................1D **35**

T

Tadley *Hants*...........................3D **11**
Tadpole Garden Village *Swin*.........1C **9**
Tadwick *Bath*.............................2C **7**
Taff's Well *Rhon*.........................1A **4**
Talaton *Devn*.............................1A **34**
Taleford *Devn*............................1A **34**
Tangley *Hants*...........................1A **20**
Tangmere *W Sus*.......................3C **33**
Taplow *Buck*.............................1C **13**
Tarnock *Som*.............................1C **15**
Tarr *Som*...................................3A **14**
Tarrant Crawford *Dors*.................3A **28**
Tarrant Gunville *Dors*..................2A **28**
Tarrant Hinton *Dors*....................2A **28**
Tarrant Keyneston *Dors*..............3A **28**
Tarrant Launceston *Dors*.............3A **28**
Tarrant Monkton *Dors*.................3A **28**
Tarrant Rawston *Dors*.................3A **28**
Tarrant Rushton *Dors*..................3A **28**
Tatling End *Buck*........................1D **13**
Tatworth *Som*...........................3C **25**
Taunton *Som*..................47 (1B **24**)
Teffont Evias *Wilts*......................1A **28**
Teffont Magna *Wilts*...................1A **28**
Tellisford *Som*............................1D **17**
Temple Cloud *Bath*.....................1B **16**
Templecombe *Som*......................1C **27**
Templeton *W Ber*.......................3A **10**
Terhill *Som*................................3A **14**
Testwood *Hants*.........................2A **30**
Tetbury *Glos*..............................1D **7**
Thakeham *W Sus*.......................2D **33**
Thames Ditton *Surr*....................3D **13**
Thatcham *W Ber*......................3C **11**
Theale *Som*..............................2D **15**
Theale *W Ber*............................2D **11**
Thickwood *Wilts*.........................2D **7**
Thorley Street *IOW*....................2A **40**
Thornbury *S Glo*.....................1B **6**
Thorncombe *Dors*......................3C **25**
Thorncombe Street *Surr*..............2C **23**
Thorne St Margaret *Som*.............1A **24**
Thorney *Som*............................1D **25**
Thorney Hill *Hants*......................1C **39**
Thornfalcon *Som*........................1B **24**
Thornford *Dors*..........................2B **26**
Thorngrove *Som*........................3C **15**
Thornhill *Cphy*............................1A **4**
Thornhill *Sotn*............................2B **30**
Thornicombe *Dors*......................3D **27**
Thorpe *Surr*..............................3D **13**
Three Legged Cross *Dors*...........3B **28**
Three Mile Cross *Wok*................3A **12**
Throop *Bour*.............................1C **39**
Thruxton *Hants*..........................2D **19**
Thurlbear *Som*..........................1B **24**
Thurloxton *Som*.........................3B **14**
Thursley *Surr*............................3C **23**
Tichborne *Hants*........................3C **21**
Tickenham *N Som*......................2D **5**
Tidcombe *Wilts*..........................1D **19**
Tiddleywink *Wilts*.......................2D **7**
Tidmarsh *W Ber*........................2D **11**
Tidpit *Hants*..............................2B **28**
Tidworth *Wilts*............................2D **19**
Tidworth Camp *Wilts*..................2D **19**
Tilehurst *Read*...........................2D **11**
Tilford *Surr*................................2B **22**
Tillington *W Sus*.........................1C **33**
Tilshead *Wilts*............................2B **18**
Timsbury *Bath*...........................1B **16**
Timsbury *Hants*.........................1A **30**

Tincleton *Dors*...........................1C **37**
Tintinhull *Som*...........................2D **25**
Tiptoe *Hants*.............................1D **39**
Tipton St John *Devn*...................1A **34**
Tisbury *Wilts*.............................1A **28**
Tisman's Common *W Sus*............3D **23**
Titchfield *Hants*..........................3C **31**
Tockenham *Wilts*........................2B **8**
Tockenham Wick *Wilts*................1B **8**
Tockington *S Glo*........................1B **6**
Todber *Dors*..............................1D **27**
Tokers Green *Oxon*....................2A **12**
Tolland *Som*.............................3A **14**
Tollard Farnham *Dors*..................2A **28**
Tollard Royal *Wilts*......................2A **28**
Toller Fratrum *Dors*....................1A **36**
Toller Porcorum *Dors*..................1A **36**
Toller Whelme *Dors*....................3A **26**
Tolpuddle *Dors*..........................1C **37**
Tonedale *Som*...........................1A **24**
Tongham *Surr*...........................2B **22**
Tongwynlais *Card*.......................1A **4**
Ton-Teg *Rhon*...........................1A **4**
Toothill *Hants*............................2A **30**
Tormarton *S Glo*........................2C **7**
Torre *Som*................................3A **14**
Tortington *W Sus*.......................3D **33**
Tortworth *S Glo*..........................1C **7**
Totland *IOW*..............................2A **40**
Totnell *Dors*..............................3B **26**
Totton *Hants*..........................2A **30**
Touchen-end *Wind*.....................2B **12**
Towns End *Hants*.......................1C **21**
Trash Green *W Ber*.....................3D **11**
Trecenydd *Cphy*.........................1A **4**
Tredogan *V Glam*.......................3A **4**
Treforest *Rhon*...........................1A **4**
Trehafod *Rhon*...........................1A **4**
Tremorfa *Card*...........................2B **4**
Trent *Dors*................................2A **26**
Tresham *Glos*............................1C **7**
Tresimwn *V Glam*.......................2A **4**
Trethomas *Cphy*.........................1A **4**
Treyford *W Sus*.........................2B **32**
Trickett's Cross *Dors*..................3B **28**
Triscombe *Som*.........................3A **14**
Trotton *W Sus*...........................1B **32**
Trowbridge *Wilts*....................1D **17**
Trowle Common *Wilts*.................1D **17**
Trudoxhill *Som*..........................2C **17**
Trull *Som*.................................1B **24**
Trumps Green *Surr*....................3C **13**
Tuckton *Bour*.............................1C **39**
Tuesley *Surr*.............................2C **23**
Tufton *Hants*.............................2B **20**
Tunley *Bath*..............................1B **16**
Tunworth *Hants*.........................2D **21**
Turfmoor *Devn*.........................3B **24**
Turgis Green *Hants*....................1D **21**
Turkey Island *Hants*...................2C **31**
Turleigh *Wilts*............................3D **7**
Turlin Moor *Pool*........................1A **38**
Turners Puddle *Dors*..................1D **37**
Turnworth *Dors*.........................3D **27**
Turville *Buck*.............................1A **12**
Turville Heath *Buck*....................1A **12**
Tutts Clump *W Ber*.....................2C **11**
Twerton *Bath*............................3C **7**
Twinhoe *Bath*............................1C **17**
Twyford *Dors*............................2D **27**
Twyford *Hants*...........................1B **30**
Twyford *Wok*.............................2A **12**
Tye *Hants*.................................3A **32**
Tyneham *Dors*...........................2D **37**
Tytherington *S Glo*......................1B **6**
Tytherington *Som*.......................2C **17**
Tytherington *Wilts*......................2A **18**
Tytherleigh *Devn*........................3C **25**

U

Ubley *Bath*................................1A **16**
Uffcott *Wilts*..............................2C **9**
Uffculme *Devn*..........................2A **24**
Uffington *Oxon*..........................1A **10**
Ufton Nervet *W Ber*....................3D **11**
Ugford *Wilts*..............................3B **18**
Ulwell *Dors*...............................2B **38**
Underwood *Newp*......................1C **5**
Undy *Mon*................................1D **5**
Upavon *Wilts*.............................1C **19**
Up Cerne *Dors*..........................3B **26**
Uphall *Dors*..............................3A **26**
Upham *Hants*............................1C **31**
Uphill *N Som*.............................1C **15**
Uploders *Dors*...........................1A **36**
Uplyme *Devn*.............................1C **35**

Up Marden *W Sus*...................................2A **32**
Up Nately *Hants*.....................................1D **21**
Upottery *Devn*.......................................3B **24**
Upper Basildon *W Ber*...........................2C **11**
Upper Bucklebury *W Ber*.......................3C **11**
Upper Bullington *Hants*.........................2B **20**
Upper Burgate *Hants*............................2C **29**
Upper Canterton *Hants*.........................2D **29**
Upper Cheddon *Som*..............................1B **24**
Upper Chicksgrove *Wilts*.......................1A **28**
Upper Church Village *Rhon*......................1A **4**
Upper Chute *Wilts*.................................1D **19**
Upper Clatford *Hants*............................2A **20**
Upper Enham *Hants*...............................2A **20**
Upper Farringdon *Hants*.........................3A **22**
Upper Froyle *Hants*................................2A **22**
Upper Godney *Som*................................2D **15**
Upper Green *W Ber*................................3A **10**
Upper Hale *Surr*....................................2B **22**
Upper Halliford *Surr*..............................3D **13**
Upper Kilcott *S Glo*..................................1C **7**
Upper Lambourn *W Ber*.........................1A **10**
Upper Langford *N Som*...........................1D **15**
Upper Minety *Wilts*.................................1B **8**
Upper Norwood *W Sus*...........................2C **33**
Upper Pennington *Hants*........................1A **40**
Upper Seagry *Wilts*.................................1A **8**
Upper Street *Hants*................................2C **29**
Upper Studley *Wilts*...............................1D **17**
Upperton *W Sus*....................................1C **33**
Upper Town *N Som*..................................3A **6**
Upper Upham *Wilts*.................................2D **9**
Upper Wield *Hants*................................3D **21**
Upper Woodford *Wilts*...........................3C **19**
Upper Wootton *Hants*............................1C **21**
Upper Wraxall *Wilts*................................2D **7**
Up Somborne *Hants*..............................3A **20**
Up Sydling *Dors*....................................3B **26**
Upton *Devn*..3A **24**
Upton *Dors*..1A **38**
.... (nr Poole)
Upton *Dors*..2C **37**
.... (nr Weymouth)
Upton *Hants*...1A **20**
.... (nr Andover)
Upton *Hants*...2A **30**
.... (nr Southampton)
Upton *IOW*..1C **41**
Upton *Oxon*...1C **11**
Upton *Slo*...2C **13**
Upton *Som*...1D **25**
Upton *Wilts*..3D **17**
Upton Cheyney *S Glo*...............................3B **6**
Upton Grey *Hants*.................................2D **21**
Upton Lovell *Wilts*.................................2A **18**
Upton Noble *Som*..................................3C **17**
Upton Scudamore *Wilts*.........................2D **17**
Upwaltham *W Sus*..................................2C **33**
Upwey *Dors*...2B **36**
Urchfont *Wilts*.......................................1B **18**
Uxbridge *G Lon*.....................................1D **13**

V
Valley End *Surr*......................................3C **13**
Vellow *Som*...3A **14**
Venn Ottery *Devn*..................................1A **34**
Ventnor *IOW*...3C **41**
Vernham Dean *Hants*.............................1A **20**
Vernham Street *Hants*...........................1A **20**
Verwood *Dors*.......................................3B **28**
Vicarage *Devn*......................................2B **34**
Virginia Water *Surr*...............................3C **13**
Vobster *Som*..2C **17**
Vole *Som*...2C **15**

W
Wadbrook *Devn*......................................3C **25**
Wadeford *Som*......................................2C **25**
Wadswick *Wilts*.......................................3D **7**
Wadwick *Hants*.....................................1B **20**
Walberton *W Sus*...................................3C **33**
Walcombe *Som*.....................................2A **16**
Walcot *Swin*..1C **9**
Walderton *W Sus*...................................2A **32**
Walditch *Dors*.......................................1D **35**
Walhampton *Hants*................................1A **40**
Walkford *Dors*......................................1D **39**
Wallingford *Oxon*...................................1D **11**
Wallington *Hants*...................................3C **31**
Wallisdown *Bour*...................................1B **38**
Walliswood *Surr*....................................3D **23**
Walterston *V Glam*..................................2A **4**
Waltham Chase *Hants*...........................2C **31**
Waltham St Lawrence *Wind*...............2B **12**
Walton *Som*..3D **15**

Walton Elm *Dors*...................................2C **27**
Walton in Gordano *N Som*........................2D **5**
Walton-on-Thames *Surr*.................3D **13**
Wambrook *Som*.....................................3B **24**
Wanborough *Surr*..................................2C **23**
Wanborough *Swin*..................................1D **9**
Wanstrow *Som*......................................2C **17**
Wantage *Oxon*......................................1B **10**
Wapley *S Glo*..2C **7**
Warblington *Hants*.................................3A **32**
Warborough *Oxon*.................................1C **11**
Wardley *W Sus*.....................................1B **32**
Wareham *Dors*......................................2A **38**
Warfield *Brac*..2B **12**
Wargrave *Wok*......................................2A **12**
Warminghurst *W Sus*.............................2D **33**
Warminster *Wilts*...........................2D **17**
Warmley *S Glo*...2B **6**
Warmwell *Dors*......................................2C **37**
Warnford *Hants*.....................................1D **31**
Warningcamp *W Sus*.............................3D **33**
Warren Corner *Hants*.............................2B **22**
.... (nr Aldershot)
Warren Corner *Hants*.............................1A **32**
.... (nr Petersfield)
Warren Row *Wind*..................................1B **12**
Warsash *Hants*.....................................3B **30**
Wash Common *W Ber*............................3B **10**
Washford *Som*......................................2A **14**
Washington *W Sus*.................................2D **33**
Watchet *Som*..2A **14**
Watchfield *Oxon*.....................................1D **9**
Waterbeach *W Sus*................................3B **32**
Waterditch *Hants*...................................1C **39**
Waterlip *Som*..2B **16**
Waterloo *Cphy*..1A **4**
Waterloo *Pool*.......................................1B **38**
Waterlooville *Hants*........................3D **31**
Waterrow *Som*......................................1A **24**
Watersfield *W Sus*.................................2D **33**
Watton *Dors*..1D **35**
Wattsville *Cphy*.......................................1B **4**
Waverley *Surr*.......................................2B **22**
Wayford *Som*..3D **25**
Waytown *Dors*.......................................1D **35**
Wealdstone *G Lon*.................................1D **13**
Weare *Som*...1D **15**
Wearne *Som*...1D **25**
Wedhampton *Wilts*.................................1B **18**
Wedmore *Som*......................................2D **15**
Weeke *Hants*..3B **20**
Welford *W Ber*......................................2B **10**
Well *Hants*..2A **22**
Well Bottom *Dors*..................................2A **28**
Wellhouse *W Ber*..................................2C **11**
Wellington *Som*...............................1A **24**
Wellow *Bath*...1C **17**
Wellow *IOW*..2A **40**
Wells *Som*.......................................2A **16**
Welton *Bath*..1B **16**
Wembdon *Som*.......................................3B **14**
Wenvoe *V Glam*.......................................2A **4**
Wepham *W Sus*.....................................3D **33**
West Amesbury *Wilts*.............................2C **19**
West Ashling *W Sus*...............................3B **32**
West Ashton *Wilts*.................................1D **17**
West Bagborough *Som*...........................3A **14**
West Bay *Dors*......................................1D **35**
West Bexington *Dors*.............................2A **36**
Westbourne *Bour*..................................1B **38**
Westbourne *W Sus*................................3A **32**
West Bradley *Som*.................................3A **16**
Westbrook *Wilts*......................................3A **8**
West Buckland *Som*...............................1A **24**
West Burton *W Sus*................................2D **33**
Westbury *Wilts*................................1D **17**
Westbury Leigh *Wilts*.............................1D **17**
Westbury on Trym *Bris*............................2A **6**
Westbury-sub-Mendip *Som*....................2A **16**
West Byfleet *Surr*..................................3D **13**
West Camel *Som*...................................1A **26**
West Chaldon *Dors*................................2C **37**
West Challow *Oxon*................................1A **10**
West Chelborough *Dors*..........................3A **26**
West Chiltington *W Sus*..........................2D **33**
West Chiltington Common *W Sus*.............2D **33**
West Chinnock *Som*...............................2D **25**
West Chisenbury *Wilts*...........................1C **19**
West Clandon *Surr*.................................1D **23**
West Coker *Som*....................................2A **26**
Westcombe *Som*.......................................3B **16**
.... (nr Evercreech)
Westcombe *Som*....................................1D **25**
.... (nr Somerton)
West Compton *Dors*...............................1A **36**
West Compton *Som*................................2A **16**
Westcot *Oxon*.......................................1A **10**

Westcott *Surr*..2D **23**
West Cranmore *Som*..............................2B **16**
West Dean *W Sus*.................................2B **32**
West Dean *Wilts*...................................1D **29**
West Drayton *G Lon*........................2D **13**
West End *Dors*......................................3A **28**
West End *Hants*....................................2B **30**
West End *N Som*.....................................3D **5**
West End *S Glo*.......................................1C **7**
West End *Surr*.......................................3C **13**
West End *Wilts*......................................1A **28**
West End *Wind*......................................2B **12**
West End Green *Hants*...........................3D **11**
Westergate *W Sus*.................................3C **33**
Westerleigh *S Glo*...................................2C **7**
Westerton *W Sus*..................................3B **32**
Westfields *Dors*.....................................3C **27**
Westford *Som*.......................................1A **24**
West Ginge *Oxon*..................................1B **10**
West Grafton *Wilts*...................................3D **9**
West Green *Hants*.................................1A **22**
West Grimstead *Wilts*.............................1D **29**
West Hagbourne *Oxon*...........................1C **11**
Westham *Dors*......................................3B **36**
Westham *Som*.......................................2D **15**
Westhampnett *W Sus*............................3B **32**
West Hanney *Oxon*................................1B **10**
West Harptree *Bath*...............................1A **16**
West Harting *W Sus*...............................1A **32**
West Hatch *Som*....................................1B **24**
Westhay *Som*.......................................2D **15**
West Heath *Hants*..................................1C **21**
.... (nr Basingstoke)
West Heath *Hants*..................................1B **22**
.... (nr Farnborough)
West Hendred *Oxon*...............................1B **10**
West Hewish *N Som*................................3C **5**
West Hill *Devn*.......................................1A **34**
West Hill *N Som*......................................2D **5**
West Holme *Dors*...................................2D **37**
West Horrington *Som*.............................2A **16**
West Horsley *Surr*.................................1D **23**
West Howe *Bour*...................................1B **38**
West Huntspill *Som*................................2C **15**
West Hyde *Herts*...................................1D **13**
West Ilsley *W Ber*..................................1B **10**
West Kennett *Wilts*..................................3C **9**
West Kington *Wilts*..................................2D **7**
West Knighton *Dors*...............................2C **37**
West Knoyle *Wilts*..................................3D **17**
West Lambrook *Som*..............................2D **25**
West Lavington *W Sus*............................1B **32**
West Lavington *Wilts*..............................1B **18**
Westleigh *Devn*.....................................2A **24**
West Littleton *S Glo*.................................2C **7**
West Lulworth *Dors*................................2D **37**
West Lydford *Som*.................................3A **16**
West Lyng *Som*.....................................1C **25**
West Marden *W Sus*..............................2A **32**
West Meon *Hants*..................................1D **31**
West Milton *Dors*...................................1A **36**
West Molesey *Surr*................................3D **13**
West Monkton *Som*................................1B **24**
West Moors *Dors*...................................3B **28**
West Morden *Dors*.................................1A **38**
West Newton *Som*.................................1B **24**
Weston *Bath*...3C **7**
Weston *Devn*...3A **24**
.... (nr Honiton)
Weston *Devn*..2A **34**
.... (nr Sidmouth)
Weston *Dors*...3B **36**
.... (nr Weymouth)
Weston *Dors*..2A **26**
.... (nr Yeovil)
Weston *Hants*.......................................1A **32**
Weston *W Ber*.......................................2A **10**
Weston Bampfylde *Som*.........................1B **26**
Westonbirt *Glos*.......................................1D **7**
Weston in Gordano *N Som*........................2D **5**
Weston Patrick *Hants*.............................2D **21**
Weston-super-Mare *N Som*.................3C **5**
Weston Town *Som*.................................2C **17**
Westonzoyland *Som*...............................3C **15**
West Orchard *Dors*................................2D **27**
West Overton *Wilts*..................................3C **9**
West Parley *Dors*...................................1B **38**
West Pennard *Som*................................3A **16**
Westport *Som*.......................................2C **25**
West Quantoxhead *Som*.........................2A **14**
Westra *V Glam*..2A **4**
West Stafford *Dors*................................2C **37**
West Stoke *W Sus*.................................3B **32**
West Stoughton *Som*.............................2D **15**
West Stour *Dors*....................................1C **27**
West Stowell *Wilts*...................................3C **9**
West Stratton *Hants*...............................2C **21**

West Thorney *W Sus*..............................3A **32**
West Tisted *Hants*.................................1D **31**
West Town *Bath*......................................3A **6**
West Town *N Som*.................................1A **42**
West Town *N Som*....................................3D **5**
West Tytherley *Hants*.............................1D **29**
West Tytherton *Wilts*................................2A **8**
West Wellow *Hants*................................2D **29**
West Wick *N Som*....................................3C **5**
West Winterslow *Wilts*............................3D **19**
West Wittering *W Sus*............................1A **42**
Westwood *Wilts*....................................1D **17**
West Woodhay *W Ber*............................3A **10**
West Woodlands *Som*.............................2C **17**
West Worldham *Hants*............................3A **22**
West Worthing *W Sus*.............................3D **33**
West Yatton *Wilts*....................................2D **7**
Wexcombe *Wilts*....................................1D **19**
Wexham Street *Buck*..............................1C **13**
Weybourne *Surr*....................................2B **22**
Weybridge *Surr*................................3D **13**
Weycroft *Devn*......................................1C **35**
Weyhill *Hants*..2A **20**
Weymouth *Dors*...............................3B **36**
Whaddon *Wilts*.....................................1C **29**
Whatley *Som*...3C **25**
.... (nr Chard)
Whatley *Som*..2C **17**
.... (nr Frome)
Wheatley *Hants*....................................2A **22**
Wheelerstreet *Surr*................................2C **23**
Wherwell *Hants*.....................................2A **20**
Whimple *Devn*.......................................1A **34**
Whippingham *IOW*.................................1C **41**
Whistley Green *Wok*...............................2A **12**
Whitchurch *Bath*......................................3B **6**
Whitchurch *Card*......................................2A **4**
Whitchurch *Hants*..................................2B **20**
Whitchurch Canonicorum *Dors*...............1C **35**
Whitchurch Hill *Oxon*.............................2D **11**
Whitchurch-on-Thames *Oxon*.................2D **11**
Whitcombe *Dors*....................................2C **37**
Whitefield *Dors*.....................................1A **38**
Whitefield *Som*.....................................1A **24**
Whitehall *Devn*......................................2A **24**
Whitehall *Hants*.....................................1A **22**
Whitehall *W Sus*....................................1D **33**
Whitehill *Hants*......................................3A **22**
White Lackington *Dors*............................1C **37**
Whitelackington *Som*..............................2C **25**
Whiteley *Hants*......................................3C **31**
Whiteley Bank *IOW*................................2C **41**
Whiteley Village *Surr*..............................3D **13**
Whitenap *Hants*.....................................1A **30**
Whiteparish *Wilts*...................................1D **29**
Whitestaunton *Som*................................2B **24**
White Waltham *Wind*..............................2B **12**
Whitfield *S Glo*...1B **6**
Whitford *Devn*.......................................1B **34**
Whitley *Wilts*..3D **7**
Whitmore *Dors*......................................3B **28**
Whitsbury *Hants*....................................2C **29**
Whitson *Newp*...1C **5**
Whittonditch *Wilts*...................................2D **9**
Whitway *Hants*......................................1B **20**
Whitwell *IOW*..3C **41**
Wick *Bour*..1C **39**
Wick *Devn*..3A **24**
Wick *Som*...2B **14**
.... (nr Bridgwater)
Wick *Som*..1C **15**
.... (nr Burnham-on-Sea)
Wick *Som*...1D **25**
.... (nr Somerton)
Wick *S Glo*...2C **7**
Wick *W Sus*..3D **33**
Wick *Wilts*..1C **29**
Wickham *Hants*.....................................2C **31**
Wickham *W Ber*.....................................2A **10**
Wickham Heath *W Ber*...........................3B **10**
Wick Hill *Wok*..3A **12**
Wick St Lawrence *N Som*.........................3C **5**
Wickwar *S Glo*..1C **7**
Widham *Wilts*..1B **8**
Widworthy *Devn*....................................1B **34**
Wigbeth *Dors*.......................................3B **28**
Wigborough *Som*...................................2D **25**
Wiggaton *Devn*.....................................1A **34**
Wiggonholt *W Sus*.................................2D **33**
Wigley *Hants*..2A **30**
Wilcot *Wilts*..3C **9**
Wildern *Hants*.......................................2B **30**
Wildhern *Hants*.....................................1A **20**
Willesley *Wilts*..1D **7**
Willett *Som*..3A **14**
Willey Green *Surr*...................................1C **23**
Williton *Som*..2A **14**

Willsbridge *S Glo* 2B **6**
Wilmington *Bath* 3B **6**
Wilmington *Devn* 1B **34**
Wilsford *Wilts* 3C **19**
.............................(nr Amesbury)
Wilsford *Wilts* 1B **18**
.............................(nr Devizes)
Wilton *Wilts* 3D **9**
.............................(nr Marlborough)
Wilton *Wilts* 3B **18**
.............................(nr Salisbury)
Wimborne Minster *Dors* 3B **28**
Wimborne St Giles *Dors* 2B **28**
Wincanton *Som* 1C **27**
Winchester *Hants* **47** (1B **30**)
Winchfield *Hants* 1A **22**
Windlesham *Surr* 3C **13**
Windmill Hill *Som* 2C **25**
Windsor *Wind* **47** (2C **1**)
Winford *IOW* 2C **41**
Winford *N Som* 3A **6**
Winfrith Newburgh *Dors* 2D **37**
Wingfield *Wilts* 1D **17**
Winkfield *Brac* 2C **13**
Winkfield Row *Brac* 2B **12**
Winklebury *Hants* 1D **21**
Winkton *Dors* 1C **39**
Winnersh *Wok* 2A **12**
Winscombe *N Som* 1D **15**
Winsham *Som* 3C **25**
Winslade *Hants* 2D **21**
Winsley *Wilts* 3D **7**
Winsor *Hants* 2A **30**
Winterborne Clenston *Dors* 3D **27**
Winterborne Herringston *Dors*...2B **36**
Winterborne Houghton *Dors*......3D **27**
Winterborne Kingston *Dors* 1D **37**
Winterborne Monkton *Dors* 2B **36**
Winterborne St Martin *Dors* 2B **36**
Winterborne Stickland *Dors* 3D **27**
Winterborne Whitechurch *Dors* ..3D **27**
Winterborne Zelston *Dors* 1D **37**
Winterbourne *S Glo* 1B **6**
Winterbourne *W Ber* 2B **10**
Winterbourne Abbas *Dors* 1B **36**
Winterbourne Bassett *Wilts* 2C **9**
Winterbourne Dauntsey *Wilts*.....3C **19**
Winterbourne Earls *Wilts* 3C **19**
Winterbourne Gunner *Wilts* 3C **19**
Winterbourne Monkton *Wilts* 2C **9**

Winterbourne Steepleton *Dors* 2B **36**
Winterbourne Stoke *Wilts* 2B **18**
Winterbrook *Oxon* 1D **11**
Winterhay Green *Som* 2C **25**
Winton *Bour* 1B **38**
Wisborough Green *W Sus* 1D **33**
Wisley *Surr* 1D **23**
Wiston *W Sus* 2D **33**
Witchampton *Dors* 3A **28**
Witham Friary *Som* 2C **17**
Witheridge Hill *Oxon* 1D **11**
Witley *Surr* 2C **23**
Wiveliscombe *Som* 1A **24**
Wivelrod *Hants* 3D **21**
Woking *Surr* 1D **23**
Wokingham *Wok* 3B **12**
Wolverton *Hants* 1C **21**
Wolverton *Wilts* 3C **17**
Wolverton Common *Hants* 1C **21**
Wonersh *Surr* 2D **23**
Wonston *Dors* 3C **27**
Wonston *Hants* 3B **20**
Wooburn *Buck* 1C **13**
Wooburn Green *Buck* 1C **13**
Woodborough *Wilts* 1C **19**
Woodbridge *Devn* 1A **34**
Woodbridge *Dors* 2C **27**
Woodcote *Oxon* 1D **11**
Woodcott *Hants* 1B **20**
Woodcutts *Dors* 2A **28**
Woodend *W Sus* 3B **32**
Woodfalls *Wilts* 1C **29**
Woodgate *W Sus* 3C **33**
Woodgreen *Hants* 2C **29**
Woodham *Surr* 3D **13**
Woodhill *N Som* 2D **5**
Woodhill *Som* 1C **25**
Woodlands *Dors* 3B **28**
Woodlands *Hants* 2A **30**
Woodlands Pk. *Wind* 2B **12**
Woodlands St Mary *W Ber* 2A **10**
Woodley *Wok* 2A **12**
Woodmancote *W Sus* 3A **32**
Woodmancott *Hants* 2C **21**
Woodmansgreen *W Sus* 1B **32**
Woodminton *Wilts* 1B **28**
Woodrow *Dors* 2C **27**
............................(nr Fifehead Neville)
Woodrow *Dors* 3C **27**
............................(nr Hazelbury Bryan)

Woodsend *Wilts* 2D **9**
Woodsford *Dors* 1C **37**
Woodshaw *Wilts* 1B **8**
Woodside *Brac* 2C **13**
Wood Street Village *Surr* 1C **23**
Woodyates *Dors* 2B **28**
Wookey *Som* 2A **16**
Wookey Hole *Som* 2A **16**
Wool *Dors* 2D **37**
Woolavington *Som* 2C **15**
Woolbeding *W Sus* 1B **32**
Woolgarston *Dors* 2A **38**
Woolhampton *W Ber* 3C **11**
Woolland *Dors* 3C **27**
Woollard *Bath* 3B **6**
Woolley *Bath* 3C **7**
Woolley Green *Wilts* 3D **7**
Woolminstone *Som* 3D **25**
Woolston *Som* 1B **26**
Woolston *Sotn* 2B **30**
Woolstone *Oxon* 1D **9**
Woolton Hill *Hants* 3B **10**
Woolverton *Som* 1C **17**
Wooth *Dors* 1D **35**
Wootton *Hants* 1D **39**
Wootton *IOW* 1C **41**
Wootton Bassett, Royal *Wilts* 1B **8**
Wootton Bridge *IOW* 1C **41**
Wootton Common *IOW* 1C **41**
Wootton Fitzpaine *Dors* 1C **35**
Wootton Rivers *Wilts* 3C **9**
Wootton St Lawrence *Hants* 1C **21**
World's End *W Ber* 2B **10**
Worlds End *Hants* 2D **31**
Worle *N Som* 3C **5**
Worminster *Som* 2A **16**
Wormley *Surr* 3C **23**
Worplesdon *Surr* 1C **23**
Worthing *W Sus* 3D **33**
Worth Matravers *Dors* 3A **38**
Worting *Hants* 1D **21**
Wortley *Glos* 1C **7**
Worton *Wilts* 1A **18**
Wotton *Surr* 2D **23**
Wotton-under-Edge *Glos* 1C **7**
Wrangway *Som* 2A **24**
Wrantage *Som* 1C **25**
Wraxall *N Som* 2D **5**
Wraxall *Som* 3B **16**
Wraysbury *Wind* 2D **13**

Wrecclesham *Surr* 2B **22**
Wrington *N Som* 3D **5**
Wroughton *Swin* 1C **9**
Wroxall *IOW* 2C **41**
Wyck *Hants* 3A **22**
Wycombe Marsh *Buck* 1B **12**
Wyfold *Oxon* 1D **11**
Wyke *Dors* 1C **27**
Wyke *Surr* 1C **23**
Wyke Champflower *Som* 3B **16**
Wyke Regis *Dors* 3B **36**
Wylye *Wilts* 3B **18**
Wymering *Port* 3D **31**
Wynford Eagle *Dors* 1A **36**

Y

Yafford *IOW* 2B **40**
Yanley *N Som* 3A **6**
Yapton *W Sus* 3C **33**
Yarcombe *Devn* 3B **24**
Yarde *Som* 3A **14**
Yarley *Som* 2A **16**
Yarlington *Som* 1B **26**
Yarmouth *IOW* 2A **40**
Yarnbrook *Wilts* 1D **17**
Yarrow *Som* 2C **15**
Yate *S Glo* 1C **7**
Yateley *Hants* 3B **12**
Yatesbury *Wilts* 2B **8**
Yattendon *W Ber* 2C **11**
Yatton *N Som* 3D **5**
Yatton Keynell *Wilts* 2D **7**
Yaverland *IOW* 2D **41**
Yawl *Devn* 1C **35**
Yeading *G Lon* 1D **13**
Yenston *Som* 1C **27**
Yeovil *Som* 2A **26**
Yeovil Marsh *Som* 2A **26**
Yeovilton *Som* 1A **26**
Yetminster *Dors* 2A **26**
Yettington *Devn* 2A **34**
Yiewsley *G Lon* 1D **13**
Ynysddu *Cphy* 1A **4**
Ynys y Barri *V Glam* 3A **4**

Z

Zeals *Wilts* 3C **17**

Published by Geographers' A-Z Map Company Limited
An imprint of HarperCollins Publishers
Westerhill Road
Bishopbriggs
Glasgow
G64 2QT

www.az.co.uk
a-z.maps@harpercollins.co.uk

HarperCollinsPublishers, Macken House, 39/40 Mayor Street Upper, Dublin 1, D01 C9W8, Ireland

13th edition 2023

© Collins Bartholomew Ltd 2023

This product uses map data licenced from Ordnance Survey
© Crown copyright and database rights 2022 OS AC0000808974

AZ, A-Z and AtoZ are registered trademarks of Geographers' A-Z Map Company Limited

A catalogue record for this book is available from the British Library.

ISBN 978-0-00-856056-0

10 9 8 7 6 5 4 3 2 1

Printed in India